"*When Women Sup[...]* [...] anyone who's ever f[...] pecially as a daughte[...] [...]ow Jess communicates her story with humor and a tangible authenticity. I was so encouraged reading this book, and I know you will be too!"

Leanna Crawford, recording artist and songwriter

"Sometimes, as women, we need to be reminded of what we bring to the table because of our Creator. We also need to be reminded that there's room for all of us at the table, and what each woman adds makes the meal even more beautiful. Grateful for these reminders in this book!"

Melinda Doolittle, recording artist

"Jessika Tate's new book is heralding the truth about the need for women to band together in unity for the advancement of the kingdom of God. It is a season of Deborahs and Esthers! Both practical and prophetic, Jessika addresses the fears, pitfalls, and obstacles that women of God can overcome to move forward into their rightful place, join the army of God, and bring the gospel to the ends of the earth."

Rev. Joanne Moody, MA, president and founder, Agape Freedom Fighters

"Jessica lives a life of championing women. She doesn't just write about it—she lives it. Her life is an example of a woman who is called to preach, to move in miracles, and to do so unapologetically, giving women a reference point for what is possible. Jessica's life has broken down barriers and forged a fresh path for women to follow in this hour. I believe this book is for such a time as this!"

Christa Smith, author and minister, Sean & Christa Smith Ministries

WHEN WOMEN SUPPORT WOMEN

Embracing God's Call to Be Yourself
and Build Ladders for Others

JESSIKA TATE

Chosen

a division of Baker Publishing Group
Minneapolis, Minnesota

Published by Chosen Books
Minneapolis, Minnesota
ChosenBooks.com

Chosen Books is a division of
Baker Publishing Group, Grand Rapids, Michigan

Printed in the United States of America

Library of Congress Cataloging-in-Publication Data
Names: Tate, Jessika, 1987– author.
Title: When women support women : embracing God's call to be yourself and build
    ladders for others / Jessika Tate.
Description: Minneapolis, Minnesota : Chosen Books, a division of Baker
    Publishing Group, [2025] | Includes bibliographical references.
Identifiers: LCCN 2024033253 | ISBN 9780800773014 (paper) | ISBN 9780800773083
    (casebound) | ISBN 9781493448869 (ebook)
Subjects: LCSH: Church work with women. | Women in church work.
Classification: LCC BV639.W7 T37 2025 | DDC 270.082—dc23/eng/20241115
LC record available at https://lccn.loc.gov/2024033253

Cover design by Faceout Studio, Molly von Borstel

Baker Publishing Group publications use paper produced from sustainable forestry practices and postconsumer waste whenever possible.

25 26 27 28 29 30 31   7 6 5 4 3 2 1

This is written for all the women who have shown me what it truly means to be a godly woman. To the biological and spiritual moms, daughters, aunts, sisters, and friends, the kingdom of God is expanding because of you. When I look at women like you, I have great hope for our future.

For my spiritual daughters, I truly believe you have the opportunity to experience a new normal for women in the body of Christ. May you fight for even more for the generation that comes after you.

Contents

Introduction

✦ ✦ ✦

If you had told me five years ago that I would be writing a book for women about women, I would have laughed at you. It was as far from my mind as writing on the scientific possibilities of exploring Mars, which I also have zero credibility to write on. For most of my ministry career I have discredited my ability to speak exclusively to women or even about women. This belief about myself most likely began long before my run-in with Christ and instead occurred in my formative years, when I identified more as a "tomboy" athlete rather than fully understanding my identity as a woman. I was only ten when my parents first had me play baseball with the boys instead of softball with the girls in our local sports league.

In today's culture I feel like I need to clarify that my parents never questioned what my actual gender was; I just happened to be a strong athlete, and they wanted me to be challenged. Times were different then, and to me this never had anything to do with my gender or sexual orientation—I genuinely assumed they were trying to protect the other girls because I could throw a ball that would take your face off if you weren't ready to catch it.

However, as I look back, I think those early years really convinced me that I didn't have much in common with other women. My personality exposed itself early on as one that was tough, stubborn, and opinionated, and I definitely preferred to lead than to follow. If given a choice to put on a dress and host a tea party, I'd rather have joined my big brother and go play absolutely anything that had a ball. My brother is only thirteen months older than I am, so in my little-girl eyes there was no one else I'd rather be like. I emulated him incessantly as a child, and now in my mid-thirties, at times I still find myself wanting to be like him in some ways. He always seemed levelheaded (except when he was angry), he was strong and respected, no one tried to run over him (except me when we were fighting), and he was and is genuinely a good person. When I, as that young, impressionable little tomboy, looked up to him, I remember thinking, "I can be tough like him."

When I fully gave my life to Jesus, He, of course, began to work on aspects of my personality that weren't like His. He compassionately dealt with those areas of my life that were "hard as nails," as my mom used to say. My mom was a ballerina and a cheerleader; in our family we call her "the crier," and she has always exhibited a tenderness that I found so difficult to attain. I had and still have a personality like my father. I couldn't always grasp my mom's ability to never meet a stranger or how she could quite literally cry at commercials that were about socks. These similarities with my dad further deepened this subconscious belief that I fit better with the boys than with the girls.

Fast-forward to my twenties, and I would do all I could to avoid women's conferences, Beth Moore Bible studies, and anything that seemed to be geared specifically toward women. When I was on staff at a church, I would serve and be kind while secretly thinking, "What, if anything, is the point to women's ministry?" I read books from John C. Maxwell, J. I. Packer, and Dallas Willard, so I dove into the leadership and theological side of ministry. I knew I was called to preach; thus, I studied the men who were preaching, and though I always seemed to have young women I was mentoring, I ultimately looked up to the male leaders in the church more than the women. When I started to do itinerate preaching, I would get invited to speak at women's meetings or conferences, and I always turned them down, usually telling God, "What would I have to say to a bunch of women?" I loved my female friends and my female leaders, but I told myself that "women's ministry just isn't my calling."

Two years ago, I moved back to the United States after almost three years of living in Brazil helping to lead a ministry school and serving in various roles in a very large denominational church. During my time there I was approached by countless young women who wanted mentoring and guidance because they felt called to lead. The denomination that church is part of does not believe women should be in ministry, though our gracious pastors often made exceptions. In spite of our leaders trying to make changes, the young women in that environment often felt overlooked, as though they were constantly hitting that glass ceiling in the church. I didn't know it then, but God was birthing a passion in me. When I came back stateside, I moved to Tennessee. I ran and still run a ministry called

Yielded Ministries, but I knew God was asking me to do something new; I just had no idea what.

I spent my first few months home fasting, praying, and if we're truly honest, begging God for direction. I felt confused. It was as if my whole life was changing in ways that I couldn't quite describe. If you've served Jesus for any measure of time, you know the feeling I'm talking about. Something in the Spirit is shifting, though you don't have the natural explanation for it. Of course, I had moved countries—that was obvious. Life and ministry were changing in so many ways that anyone could see on the surface, but there was more happening under the surface, in my heart, that I just couldn't quite pinpoint. Then one day God made it so clear: I was going to start focusing on women.

When He spoke, I immediately burst into tears. I don't know if it was because of His presence, because of clarity, or because my biggest ministry nightmare was coming true. I was going to minister to women. I mean, by this age I had dated, I liked to have my nails done, and I was a sucker for a good ol' women's small group, but I still wasn't ready to narrow my focus so intentionally. If I'm really honest with you and with myself, as an unmarried woman in my thirties, though I'd worked through so many of the doubts I had about myself, I still felt largely unqualified to minister to women due to my marital status. If this was Jesus, which I felt it was, I had to chalk it up to God truly choosing the foolish and the weak (1 Corinthians 1:27–31).

This book has come about because in this time of ministering to women, I have become so convinced of God's heart toward women in the church. I am overwhelmed and undone by His heart, not only in how He loves us but in how He desires that we lead. I believe women have an integral role in the church and that this has largely been misunderstood by both men and women. I, like all of us, have noticed that many times it is women who can be so horribly awful to one another. We have heard the stereotypes that we are jealous, competitive, and gossipy. I am tired of hearing that women don't support each other. I believe that when women support women, we are absolutely unstoppable.

So this book is for you, dear sister, with the hope that you would step into all that God has called you to be. My prayer is that you would not shrink back, you would not play small, and ultimately, you would not give in to the attacks and temptations of the Enemy, but instead you would fully embrace and fulfill all that God has destined you to be. That you would choose to be a woman who allows herself to be supported and chooses to radically support other women. Together we can change the narrative, and we can change the future.

1

The Greatness of a Woman

What, sir, would the people of the earth be without woman? They would be scarce, sir, almighty scarce. Then let us cherish her; let us protect her; let us give her our support.

Mark Twain, address at the Washington
Correspondents' Club, 1868

When I was in middle school, years before I met Jesus, our teacher assigned us *The Hiding Place*, by Corrie ten Boom. If you aren't familiar with Corrie's story, she and her family hid Jews in their house in the Netherlands during World War II. After being caught, Corrie's family was sent off to the concentration camps, where every member of her family except her eventually would succumb to death. Corrie told in-depth stories about her time in the camp, including miraculous tales of God's provision as well as her and her sister Betsie's own self-sacrifice to benefit absolute strangers. I'll never forget Betsie willingly sharing a jar of medicine that she so desperately needed with all the other women in their barracks. Story after story, the two sisters demonstrated such great faith in God while in the midst of arguably some of the worst darkness the world has ever experienced. In persecution, they continually chose gratefulness and generosity. As a young teenager I was deeply impacted by Corrie's story. I can vividly recall thinking to myself as I read their story, "One day I want to do something great too." Betsie and Corrie gave such an impeccable example of how women can support women.

For as long as I can remember, I felt a yearning for greatness. As a young athlete I had grand dreams of hitting the winning three-point shot at the buzzer to win the game. When I started baking, I knew I would make the best chocolate chip cookie the world had ever tasted. It didn't matter what realm of life or even my absolute lack of talent in the area. Whatever I was doing, I wanted to be great. I remember as a child having the tenacity to do more than what people thought I could. I no doubt had the "anything you can do, I can do better" mentality. It never occurred to me that these ideas were far-fetched. I genuinely believed I was born for greatness. As I write this book at the prime age of thirty-six, I'd still say that I believe you and I were born for something great with God. Oh sure, some of our childhood desires were misguided, to say the least—cue your memories of the various aspirations you had as a child. God has many times had to purify and refine what greatness is for all of us. Still, that thing that has been inside of you since you were young, unaware of cultural norms, and oblivious to potential limitations or prerequisites, I actually believe was placed there by

God. Today, as you read this, if that fire inside that little girl still exists, even if it's been almost extinguished and is now just a tiny little flame, I think you're reading this because God wants to pour gasoline on that fire.

When I met Jesus at sixteen, my innate desire to basically be awesome didn't really stop; it just shifted. The longing to overcome and exceed expectations simply found a new outlet. I no longer wanted to be in the WNBA (yes, this was actually once a deep desire of mine with every centimeter of my five-foot-six frame). I just decided I was going to be the best daughter God had ever seen. I was going to study the Bible nonstop, learn all the theology things, find a way to have third-heaven encounters, and be Joyce Meyer, but even better. (Joyce, if by some sovereign moment you're reading this, I apologize.) I believe every single one of us has an innate desire placed by God inside of us to be great. You can recall that urging inside of you that told you that you weren't created just to exist; you were born for more. Within these desires, both the refined and unrefined, there are often countless obstacles, disappointments, flat-out betrayals, and even unimaginable moments of wishing that the longing might quiet down so you could just be normal, whatever that is supposed to mean. Who knew that any attempt to do more than just the ordinary would face an all-out assault?

Regrettably, within the church we find the most backlash. The beautiful church with all its diversity has not quite come to an agreement on how it feels about women, especially women who stand out. It is easy to see that men seem to be the "great" ones, both inside and outside the church. We might have had Mother Teresa and Rosa Parks or even Beth Moore. Still, every single American president in our country's history has been male, as well as cultural challengers like Martin Luther King Jr., athletes like Michael Jordan and Babe Ruth, pioneers like Neil Armstrong, and evangelists like Billy Graham and Reinhard Bonnke. It isn't hard to find masculine role models. They have always seemed to be the leaders in every aspect of society. I don't know at what age I began to recognize the proverbial glass ceilings that are present in society, but I've always known that I was willing to do whatever it took to go after more in my life. I want more than just average for myself, for you, and for my spiritual kids, and if there are glass ceilings, well, let's just shatter them. Let's be and raise the next generation of female role models. To reconcile this in society both in and out of the church, we need women who will support each other. We cannot accomplish this task alone.

Admittedly, in the church it often feels way more complicated than just a glass ceiling. It appears to be a much deeper issue than that. In fact, in the church I attended when I was saved, most people truly believed that God only created women to make babies and support men in their God-given assignments to lead. Being a wife and a mother is a noble and important calling, but women's callings are not one-size-fits-all, and God has created each woman for a unique purpose—and many of the purposes do not fit the "normal" paradigm some churches and Christians have. Because I am a single woman at thirty-six, my calling has looked much different from that of my friend who is a stay-at-home mom of seven. We need to rid ourselves of the stereotypes and stipulations around what following Jesus means for each individual woman.

Over the years I have heard countless stories of women who have had less than desirable experiences in the church when they decided to believe they were born for more than what felt "normal." If you are like me, then you don't mind the idea of shattering glass ceilings, but you certainly don't want to go to war with God. Many women all over the globe love Jesus with every fiber of their being and desire more than anything else to love Him well. Even if that means learning to wear dresses more regularly, keeping their opinions to themselves, and serving on the church's kitchen team, ultimately changing so much of who they are, then they would be willing.

But what if you aren't normal? What if you don't fit the mold? When you look around at the church or perhaps even other women, maybe it sometimes feels like you were just made different. What if this was actually all by the grand design of the one who made you?

At times, being a woman still feels convoluted. There seems to be a set of rules and regulations that we never quite received the memo on. Culture changes its demands all too often, and it is easy to get whiplash trying to keep up. When I met Jesus for the first time, I felt so overwhelmingly accepted. The realization that He knew every part of me and still loved me, still wanted me, and still chose me was truly life altering. As a teenager I had been hoping some man would accept me as the woman I was. Even though I had dated some, I still always felt like I was only truly accepted when I changed who I was. When I decided to be a little more like everyone else and quite a lot less like me, I guess. Then Jesus came into the story. His love isn't conditional, and I did absolutely nothing to earn it. There is most definitely a process, but over time, I began to realize that it genuinely is He who made me. And He didn't just make me like some random luck of the draw, but He made me *Imago Dei*, literally in His image. The same is true for you—He is the one who designed you piece by piece, even those parts you may have felt didn't make sense.

Now, please understand I am not advocating God's total approval of every decision we make. I am certainly not condoning sin. What I am saying is that so many of us live our lives feeling like God must have made a mistake with us. That somehow the creator of the universe, in all His power, surely didn't recognize that some of us women aren't supposed to be the way we are. I am suggesting that perhaps, my friend, we have been lied to, that you and I were intricately designed how He wanted us to be.

Maybe God, in His incredible sovereignty, knew what He was doing when He made you and has a plan for even those parts of you that don't seem to fit just right. Imagine that He wanted to use some of that tenacity built into you, or perhaps your quiet, soft demeanor. He has a plan for how your heart thrives in challenge and even some of that stubbornness too. You simply need to find how God wants to use those attributes. As you step into all that God has called you to be, you will find that even those characteristics you have despised about yourself He has deliberately placed inside of you for His unique purposes.

It is in Christ and Christ alone that you will find the healing, solace, and clarity your heart so desperately cries out for. It is in Him that you will find the outlet for that deep desire for more than what you think is possible, and in Him, permission is granted for you to fully embrace the person, the minister, the woman you were created to be.

Elisabeth Elliot is a woman who deeply inspires me. When she had every right to give up, she chose not to. Elisabeth is an outstanding example to all of us of what is possible when we find true healing in Christ. Elisabeth and her husband, Jim, lived as missionaries ministering to the indigenous people of Ecuador. In 1956 her husband and four friends were speared to death by a tribe they were going to minister to. After Jim's death, Elisabeth continued to minister in Ecuador and studied the language of the tribe that had killed her husband. About two years later, she went with her then-three-year-old daughter to bring the gospel to the tribe, and she lived among them for two years.[1] Elliot did not allow these challenges to keep her from what God had called her to do. I don't think any of us would have blamed her for taking her little girl and just returning to the comforts of home in the United States, but she refused to settle for what would have been comfortable. Elisabeth did not let her pain and disappointment hold her back. She forged ahead, trusting the one who had called her.

The journey to do something great is undoubtedly filled with enormous highs and lows. No one ever did anything great by playing small or giving in to doubts. Some of the most tremendous aches in my heart still come as I travel all over the world, meeting women who have yet to find that same permission and freedom to just be the women God created them to be. Often, I find these women not in the patriarchal religions in other parts of the world that inherently despise women, but right here, in my own tribe, in the Christian church. In this place where you should be encouraged the most to flourish and grow into your potential. Here in the same church where our Jesus chose to come to earth, born of a woman.

Now it is His body that often stifles the same women He went out of His way to protect and empower. The church should not be the place where you feel most afraid to shine; instead, it should be the place where you receive the greatest amount of support. We as women should provide support as spiritual sisters to the women around us. The church should be the place where your sisters actually hold your feet to the fire, insisting that you refuse to be anything less than what God designed you to be. I am holding your feet to the fire today. I am telling you there is more inside of you than what you have realized. If God is calling you to it, then it is time to stop disqualifying yourself.

To be completely honest, I never thought I would do women's ministry. I reflect on the majority of my life and still think I am the last woman I would choose for this assignment. Doubts still try to sneak in for every new thing God launches me into.

It is so familiar for us to disqualify ourselves. We think that God must have at least a thousand other women who would be better suited for the exact assignment God has given us. The problem is, God didn't give them the assignment; He gave it to us. The more we let go of the reasons why not, the more we can embrace the "why not now?" mentality. Our healing and our freedom are meant to set other captives free. What is the world missing out on because we've disqualified ourselves?

Due to so much controversy around the role of a woman in the home, in the church, and in society, countless women have yet to find their voice. Over and over again, as I speak in churches and conferences, I have a line of women waiting for me after a session, each with her own story of knowing deep inside that there is more for her. Each has felt the call of God on her life and can't shake the stirring of Holy Spirit urging her to press through the adversity.

We have an incalculable number of women today who live in the shadows of society's expectations. For those women who just so happen to dare to be extraordinary, there is an unending line of blockades that meet them, determined to force them back into compliance.

This is not my attempt to write a "woe is me" woman's book. Actually, it is quite the opposite. This is my urgent appeal to you reading this book: to believe, to be set free, and to not just step into the fullness of your calling but champion other women to do the same. May we, as women, together alongside men, truly become all that God has called us to be. From our homes to the pulpits, let us fulfill our destiny.

If history does indeed repeat itself, many will criticize the women who believe for more, the ones who choose not to settle and instead pursue a higher calling. Take, for instance, the women's suffrage movement. Women like Susan B. Anthony fought hard against much resistance to win the right to vote for women in the United States. When Anthony first voted in the presidential election of 1872, she was arrested and convicted. It might seem appalling today that there would be such massive resistance around something as simple as women voting, but at the time there was immense persecution from both men and women. Suffragists were ridiculed in the media and sometimes attacked physically. Even pastors took to their pulpits to stand against those who aligned with the suffragist movement. Entire organizations were formed to oppose the suffragist agenda. Anti-suffragists assumed that most women did not even want to vote or be involved in politics at all. Some had the audacity to argue that women did not have the mental capacity to vote rationally or have an informed opinion. Society itself turned on the women who dared believe for more. They refused to lightly consider that women, like men, had a God-given destiny, that women were also created in God's image and given a plan and a purpose.

There continue to be plenty of Christian men *and* women who believe that women should just stay silent and remain in the background. All too often, the harshest critics of world-changing women are found in the church. We will tackle the biblical perspectives of women in the next chapter because we do not want to be ignorant of what the Bible says about women or ignore passages that feel difficult. But when it is looked at in context, we can see that the Bible celebrates women. Jesus consistently broke cultural norms to empower women. There has recently been a wave of well-known leaders in the church repenting for not doing their due diligence concerning what God has to say about women. Many have come to recognize that God, indeed, does have a destiny for women beyond what the church has deemed acceptable.

We need women. We need wives, moms, daughters, and aunts to embrace the call of God on their lives. The facts are biologically quite simple, despite what culture has tried to convince us: Only biological women can give birth to humanity. I haven't yet birthed a child biologically, though I am thankful for spiritual children whom I love like my own. I have not had the unique privilege of carrying a child in my womb. I do not experientially know the weight of caring for a tiny little human who is 100 percent dependent on me. What I am told is there is absolutely not a single moment of the day when you forget there is a child inside of you. You hold the responsibility in mind at all times, and everything you do is in some way affected by the baby you carry. Then a day comes when you embrace the pain of birthing for the joy of holding that child in your arms.

One thing I know for sure is that women can do hard things. We are not weak or frail. When the motivation is there, we can do what seems impossible. Having never birthed a child before, the thought of enduring the awkwardness and pain of shoving a tiny little baby out of my, um, lower parts feels utterly impossible, yet countless women all around the world have endured this very thing. And many of them, and possibly you, have chosen to do this not only once but multiple times.

When I think about doing hard things, I consider so many of the women before us who have dared to be great. We are all well acquainted with Amelia Earhart, but have you heard of Geraldine Mock? Amelia decided that she would be the first woman to fly around the globe, obviously not achieving that feat, as Amelia is better known for her disappearance during her attempt. Before her fateful final flight, Amelia said, "Women must try to do things as men have tried. When they fail, their failure must be but a challenge to others."[2] Geraldine Mock is the woman who was so challenged by the failure of Earhart that she actually became the first woman to fly around the world. As Geraldine was taking off for her journey, she heard the air traffic controller remark, "Well, I guess that's the last we'll hear from her."[3] Make no mistake about it, what Mock was attempting was difficult: a grueling twenty-nine-day trip flying solo to do what no woman had done before. She embraced the uncertainty for the opportunity to do something great.

Don't tell me that women, when properly motivated, can't do hard things. We *can* do hard things. We know how to be unselfish, loving, and merciful. We know how to self-sacrifice for the benefit of others. To put it directly, we carry within us naturally so many attributes of our Jesus.

Yet choosing to break out of the mold takes work. Prioritizing healing so that we can be healthy for the next generation can be challenging. Giving God a radical yes that goes beyond just familiar Christianity, well, that's not easy either, but we can do it. We can do it together.

Let me be so blatantly clear. I believe we are in a unique time for women in the body of Christ. I can feel it in my bones. God hasn't only spoken to me about this; there are other leaders and prophets in the body of Christ all over the world who are saying the same. God is releasing a unique grace for women. He is metaphorically sending out the "bat signal" to His daughters. It is time—the moment for us to relinquish all the excuses and give God our absolute yes. It is time for women to recognize that, just as Esther, we were born for such a time as this (Esther 4:14).

Most likely you know her story. Esther was an orphan who found favor with the king. She was divinely placed in a specific place at a specific time so that she could help bring about the rescue of her people from death. Esther would have to violate tradition and break out of the ordinary, risking her life so that she could fulfill her God-given destiny. It is not difficult to understand why Esther was reluctant. It takes substantial courage to risk your own life for the sake of another. We can skim over this story, nodding our heads and giving an "amen" without acknowledging the true depth of trust in God and self-less bravery Esther's actions required. Yet her heroism saved an entire people group. Esther was born for just that moment.

In 2023, I attended a gathering of prophetic leaders. None of them had consulted with each other before they came to share what they felt God was saying for the season. Now, understand, this wasn't a women's conference. This was a prophetic conference for the general body of Christ. One by one, however, almost every single speaker addressed the need for godly women to fully yield to the plans of God for their lives. One respected prophetic leader said specifically that God was bringing healing to women so that they could embrace their God-ordained identity in their churches.

I am not believing to see a quasi-feminist movement wreak havoc in the church, as secular feminism has attempted to do; however, I am boldly believing for a fresh wave of women who refuse to shrink back in this season. I am praying for fiery mama bears who will not be content to watch as culture takes a devastating turn against healthy families. I am desperate to see a generation of women who will rise above the petty issues that have so often pitted women against each other, and instead, I am calling on us to stand together for ourselves, our families, and the next generation.

As I have said and will continue to say, it is time. Friend, woman of God, it is time. As Paul encouraged the Corinthian church, it is time that we put our childish ways behind us and move forward into the call of God on our lives. More than ever, we need you. We need you to say yes to Him. Say yes to casting off your old, nasty flesh and to pursuing true godliness, purity, and love. We need you to be so filled with Holy Spirit that the fear of man is put to death in you. We need you to embrace that nudge in your gut telling you there is more. Now is the time to boldly enter in.

I am writing this book because I believe in you. There is far more than you imagined on the other side of your yes. I know that there is a generation of young women who are praying and hoping for someone just like you. They are searching for the women who are willing to say yes to something bigger. They need your example. They need to have what you likely did not have: a culture of women who will support other women as we all work together to see God's plan unfold in our generation.

During the Holocaust, a Polish social worker by the name of Irena Sendler decided she could not idly sit back and watch as Jews were being sent off to concentration camps to face certain torture and death. Irena was determined to intervene, and she helped set in motion a secret mission to rescue many Jewish children. She not only risked her life to save the lives of others but also convinced many other women to do the same. Her secret network helped smuggle Jewish children out and then forged documents to place the children inside Polish homes, orphanages, and even convents, where they would be safe from the Nazis. Throughout the war, it is said that Irena helped to rescue over 2,500 children. The German occupiers eventually uncovered Sendler's work in the Polish underground, and the Gestapo came to arrest her. Sendler endured severe torture yet never revealed any details about the network or the location of any of the hidden children. By a miracle, Irena survived her torture, and though she was sentenced to death, she was released from her imprisonment. Irena's story was not told for over sixty years; finally the details began to be released about her numerous selfless acts of bravery to benefit others. She later said of herself, "Heroes do extraordinary things. What I did was not an extraordinary thing. It was normal."[4]

So often, I find myself telling women, "You weren't born to be 'normal'; you were born to be extraordinary." But perhaps Irena is right. Maybe we simply need to redefine what it means to be normal. A normal Christian. A normal woman. I pray that as we journey through this book together, we will decide to step into Irena's normal. A normal that may not feel so normal for most of us right now. A normal where women encourage each other. A normal where other women see the greatness inside of you and champion you into your God-given purpose. This normal is where women build ladders for the women around them instead of trying to trip them. You may not have experienced this normal yet, but together we can create it for all the women in the body of Christ. A normal where women support other women.

2

Women and the Church

When we denigrate a woman, we are in fact diminishing part of the image of God.... When we put women down, we tarnish the image of God.

Christine Caine, *Unashamed*

The church should be the safest place for every human being to be free to embrace their God-given destiny. My spiritual father rightfully calls churches "destiny incubators." If God has a uniquely designed purpose for each and every one of us, then it is obvious that His church should facilitate, or at a bare minimum encourage, those purposes into fruition. Unfortunately, for most of us, that has not been the case. The theological confusion around certain passages concerning gender roles, as well as generations of strict patriarchal leadership, has often confined women to limiting positions both in the home and in the church.

A few months ago I made a little post on Instagram, or as my friend affectionately calls it, "SIN-stagram," where I made a comment affirming women preachers. Within minutes it felt like I had taken a baseball bat to a beehive. The comments were raging, mostly accusatory toward those of us who allow women to be in the pulpit, saying that we have decided to completely disregard the Bible and make up our own rules. I was not shocked at all by the comments that came barreling in. Having been a woman preacher for eighteen years now, these opinions aren't foreign to me. Rather, I was shocked by who was writing the bulk of the comments. It appeared the majority of these hateful and, quite frankly, ignorant comments were coming from . . . women. I am well accustomed to men who want to ensure that women stay in their "rightful place" (please note my sarcasm), but I was in more shock than those boys who watched Enoch disappear into the sky. This harsh criticism was coming from *sisters*!

Upon chatting with other female friends, both those in the ministry and those who are not, I found a similar consensus: It is women who are often the cruelest and most hateful when it comes to other women attempting to rise above what their church has deemed a woman's rightful place. Although many men have no doubt chosen to theologically manipulate women into some sort of distorted submission, it appears that it is women who have become the most condemning of their fellow women. This is disheartening, to say the least. For women to truly become all that God has called them to be, we need women supporting women, not just in their roles as wives or mothers, but in any endeavor God has set before them. I suppose that for women to really support other women, we need to start with an accurate understanding of what Scripture says about women.

As we proceed with this chapter, I want to be clear that I am not a bra-burning feminist or even adamantly against traditional gender roles. In fact, I write this with the fear of God and the conviction that it isn't so much about what I am against, but rather what I am for. I am pro the proper interpretation of biblical passages. I am not an accredited theologian, nor do I claim to be. At the time I am writing this, I am about to begin my doctorate in ministry, and all that really means is I have become increasingly aware of how many supersmart people are out there studying the Bible. Being surrounded by lots of people smarter than me throughout my schooling, I prefer to leave the parsing of the Hebrew and Greek texts to those who have dedicated their lives to that purpose; however, I am eager to study for myself and lean on the brilliance of others as well.

I care deeply about the heart of the Father being correctly communicated through His living Word, so in this chapter we will look at passages from the Bible to see what Scripture as a whole teaches about women and also lean on some of those smart people to help us understand those passages. In addition to my deep passion for Scripture, I am also an extreme advocate for both men and women fulfilling their God-given purposes in spite of anyone else's opposing opinions. Thus, this chapter is an attempt to dive into the heart of Jesus as revealed in Scripture and shed perspective on what we've been told about the Bible and women.

I am not trying to convince you, but I do want to open your eyes to the possibility that we have been taught a face-value interpretation of verses that were never meant to be understood with such cursory inspection. Instead of attempting to truly understand these verses in light of the context of Jesus' character and interactions with women, we have often just taken these verses as swords to shut down and shut up an entire gender. Even famed evangelical pastor Rick Warren has admitted that in his fifty-three years of ministry, he had never done a proper exegesis of the passages he had personally used to keep women silent and out of leadership in his church.[1] If he can humbly admit that publicly, knowing the backlash that he would and did receive, then we can certainly do our due diligence before hurling more insults at women who just want to obey God, whether that is as a wife, mother, sister, minister, or CEO.

Here is my plea to you, my friend: Even as we look at a new perspective on these verses, no matter how you choose to interpret them, please do not use the Bible as a sword to slice and dice your fellow sisters. As Sarah Bessey says, "I have learned the difference between critical thinking and just being critical."[2] My prayer is that this chapter, or even this book for that matter, would not cause you to be critical, but rather, it would challenge you to think critically about what the Scripture is actually communicating and how God demonstrates the ways in which we should be supporting women.

Understanding someone's history helps us to grasp their framework for certain perspectives. My framework for women in the church was blown to smithereens by God Himself. I had an encounter with God at seventeen years old that would forever challenge what I had been taught about women. I can close my eyes, and in an instant I am taken back to that old Baptist church in my small hometown. I had only recently become a Christian, and the hunger for Him I was experiencing was more than I could comprehend. I would sneak over to the church after school on days I didn't have some sort of sports practice and slip into the empty sanctuary. Most days I was completely at a loss for what I was doing there; I just knew I wanted to be as close as possible to where I thought the presence of God was. In some odd way, I felt drawn to the room. It sat a few hundred people on green chairs attached to one another in row after row. I would circle the empty chairs along the side of the wall, make my way to the back, and then circle again, but I never made my way up the stairs to the altar area where the pulpit was. It felt like sacred space that was best left untouched. I would make my circles and at times sit down on the floor, where I had shed more tears than could be counted during Sunday morning worship and altar calls.

During one of these afternoons I was walking and praying when God spoke to me and told me to go up the stairs and stand behind the pulpit. Just the thought of it made me weak in my knees. By the time I reached the stairs, I was basically crawling as I made my way over to the large wooden pulpit. I stood up, gripping the sides with both hands to keep my knees from buckling.

As I stood in this spot, which to me was reserved for the holy, the ordained, and most definitely the men, God clearly spoke to me. He said, "Jessika, you will preach to more people than can fit in this room."

Since I was a strong female, you would think I'd yell out a good ol' Southern "Hallelujah!" Instead I became absolutely terrified. I looked around the room and thought, "Me?" as if someone else had happened to sneak into the room and God had mistakenly confused our assignments. My next thought came barreling through like a bulldozer. "Wait. Did He say preach?" I was young in the Lord and fairly new to this hearing-God thing, but it had been so clear, I couldn't deny it. Then reality began to sink in. Not only did He say preach, but He said I would "preach to more people than could fit in the room." At the time, the thought of speaking to even half of that room seemed absolutely ludicrous and terrifying. I could have possibly wrapped my head around a small youth Bible study, but even that was way beyond what I was comfortable with.

That's the day when, as I stood there gripping that pulpit, God violated my theology. You have likely had at least one similar moment in your own journey with Him—an experience when you found out God was different from what you thought or even how you had been taught. I would have been the first one to jump on the train of stone throwers telling Beth Moore or Lisa Bevere to get out of the pulpit. No doubt in my zeal for Him I would have mistakenly but purposefully rebuked fellow women. The truth was, at that time I didn't know any better. I truly believed I was defending Scripture by condemning women who I thought were treating it like suggestions. Maybe that was once you, or maybe that is you now; either way, it is far past time we deal with this issue.

For women to move forward into their God-given identities, we need to settle the biblical issues around passages that appear to limit them. We cannot deny that Paul wrote that women should remain silent in the church. There is no debate that these passages exist; however, it is extremely possible, and it is my belief, that there is plenty to be discussed as to the context and implications of these writings. Did Paul intend that his words would restrict women from certain leadership roles in the church for the lifetime of the church?

When studying the Bible, context is key. For example, Paul also wrote that women should make sure their heads are covered, but very few churches have monitors at the door inspecting our haircuts (1 Corinthians 11:14–15). If they did, I am not sure what we are supposed to do with women who go through chemotherapy and lose their hair. If we take this passage literally and apply it universally, then women who are battling cancer and lose their hair with treatment are a disgrace. I know several people close to me who have walked through this exact situation and lost all their hair, so this implication is grieving to me. I have been perplexed that the same men who wouldn't let women teach in their churches because of Paul's words have no problem letting their wives braid their hair and wear their big ol' Texas bling necklaces when Paul clearly admonished women to dress modestly, without costly clothing or braided hair (1 Timothy 2:9–10). Perhaps the ideology around women in leadership would not be so frustrating to me if we took each of these passages with the same measure of dogma. Though I disagree with the interpretation, I could stomach it a little better if it were consistent, rather than appearing to pick and choose which passages to strictly enforce and which can be loosely applied.

Before we dive into a few of the well-known verses that have been used to limit women, I want to take note of what we see from Jesus first. Jesus came to reveal to us the King and His kingdom. Hebrews 1:3 tells us that Jesus is the exact imprint of the nature of God. If you want to know God's heart, then look no further than the life of Jesus. Despite the patriarchal culture of the day, Jesus consistently went out of His way to support women, even when it had the potential to cause Him rejection or even prosecution. It is one of the most beautiful things about Him, that He was willing to quite literally take on the shame of women at His own expense in an extremely patriarchal culture.

This is just one of the many things I love about Jesus. He was never intimidated by societal pressure or cultural norms. Jesus intentionally violated the theology of the religious to reveal to them the heart of the Father that they had been missing. He didn't mind touching the leper so that those around Him would see the truth of the kingdom. As Bill Johnson says, "Under the Old Testament, if you touch a leper, you become unclean. . . . But in the New Testament we touch a leper and the leper becomes clean."[3] Jesus didn't just proclaim, He demonstrated this wild, upside-down, turn-you-inside-out, boggle-your-mind kingdom that we have the privilege of being part of. He was a revolutionary, especially when it came to women.

In order to understand just how countercultural He was, we have to step out of our Western mindsets. Kenneth Bailey is a leading scholar in Middle Eastern and New Testament studies. In his book *Jesus through Middle Eastern Eyes*, Bailey tells us that men and women in the Middle Eastern culture of Jesus' day—and in some cultures today—were not to speak to strangers of the opposite gender. In fact, rabbis would not even speak to females from their own family when out in public.[4] There were very clear lines dividing the genders, and many of those lines still exist today in conservative areas. When I was doing missions in the Middle East, we women were instructed to never approach a man in public. These gender lines have been in place for generations, and to dare to cross them can put you or your family at risk.

Then, right in the middle of this conservative culture, along comes Jesus, who was never phased by the lines men had drawn. In John 4 we see Jesus intentionally walk up and start a conversation with a Samaritan woman. Oops! Didn't He know that He shouldn't even talk to His mother in public, much less a female stranger? Oh, but our Jesus, He takes it even further, as He tends to do. He doesn't just approach her—He even asks her for a drink. He now puts Himself in a place of vulnerability to a woman, and not just any woman, but a Samaritan stranger. This is so astounding that even the disciples are baffled by what He's doing (John 4:27). Jesus takes one culturally inappropriate conversation with a woman He should never even be talking to, and He turns her into a successful evangelist (John 4:39). Jesus obviously disagreed with the cultural position of women and had no problem breaking the perceived rules to exemplify the heart of God for women.

Beyond this astonishing evangelistic conversation, Jesus does something even crazier in Luke 10:38–42, when He allows Mary to come and sit at His feet. At first glance this may simply seem to be a kind gesture from the loving Messiah, but with a deeper look we can see this would have been flat-out offensive to the religious leaders of the day. For a little perspective, first-century teacher Rabbi Eliezer said, "Let the words of the Torah be burnt, before being handed over to a woman."[5]

In direct contrast to Rabbi Eliezer, Jesus allows Mary to sit and learn at His feet (Luke 10:39). To sit at a teacher's feet as Mary did is to take the posture of a disciple. At the time women were occasionally allowed to listen to a rabbi's teachings, but they most definitely would never have been found sitting in a disciple's position at the feet of a rabbi.[6] I bet if we could jump into this scene, we could probably have cut the tension in the air with a knife. We should acknowledge that it is Martha who verbally complains to Jesus about Mary. It wasn't the men in the room—it was Mary's friend; it was her sister. Martha is the one to first be frustrated by Mary's attempt to break out of normalcy. As we can sense from the text, Martha wants to shout at Mary, "Don't you know your place?" It is as if Martha, a woman, is frustrated not just because her sister isn't helping her but because she has the audacity to think she has the right to sit among the men. For sure, everything Mary was doing in this moment was against what was culturally appropriate.

We do not get to hear this side of the story in the Bible text, but I would imagine in this moment that Martha is not the only one dreaming of smacking Mary right across her bold face. Every other man and woman in that room would be thinking, "Who in the name of everything holy does this woman think she is?" Not only was Mary neglecting what would be considered her rightful female duties—even Martha thought so—but she was also bla-tantly violating the cultural and religious structures of the day. Women were not to be sitting in that room with the men. The women were to be in the kitchen, and the men were to be learning from the rabbi.

And Jesus, our sweet Jesus, defends Mary—not just to Martha, but to every man sitting in that room. Jesus says to Martha, in front of everyone, "Mary has chosen what is better, and it will not be taken away from her" (Luke 10:42 NIV). Some translations say, "Mary has chosen the *good* part." The Greek word for "good" or "better" is *agathos*, which, according to *Vine's Expository Dictionary*, can literally be translated as "morally good or pleasing to God." In other words, Mary chose the right thing according to God.

This passage is loaded for us women. I could easily digress from our topic at hand as Jesus demonstrates to us that being a disciple, even as a woman, is the correct pathway. Before serving and setting the table, even before culturally acceptable stereotypes, our place as women is to be His disciples. Not always in the kitchen or on the hospitality team, but right there with the men learning from our Savior. It is the good place. It is the right place. Jesus breaks every cultural rule to let us know that we aren't supposed to be put in the side room while the men learn how to be disciples; we are supposed to be right up in the mix of all of it, close to Him. As Katia Adams states in her book *Equal*, "Discipleship was not just about learning. It was about learning *in order to become like the rabbi Himself*" (emphasis in the original).[7] Jesus didn't simply allow Mary to become a disciple in this moment, He commended it, and thus He empowered Mary to take a position that was previously only meant for men. Did you catch that? He didn't just tolerate Mary's boldness, He publicly championed her in it.

These are just two scenarios where Jesus reveals God's heart for women. Ladies, we need not discredit one another if this is how He feels about us. We must take our cue from our Lord and support other women. There is no way to take Scripture and argue theologically that Jesus wanted women to stay in a subservient position. Most who take this position will ignore the life of Jesus and focus on the words of Paul. I would suggest that it's extremely dangerous to ignore the perspective of Jesus in any of our theology, but nonetheless, let us look at a few of these difficult passages. Due to space, we cannot look at every verse on this topic, but I want to hit a few of the main ones.

> Now I commend you because you remember me in everything and maintain the traditions even as I delivered them to you. But I want you to understand that the head of every man is Christ, the head of a wife is her husband, and the head of Christ is God.
>
> 1 Corinthians 11:2–3

This set of verses in 1 Corinthians has been used by complementarians to tell women that their primary role in the home, in the church, and in society is one of ultimate submission. The verbiage used is meant to express that though women are equal in value, we are lesser in the realm of leadership qualities, wisdom, our ability to hear God—and the list goes on and on. The message to women has been clear for generations: In theory, you have the same value as men, but we cannot possibly allow you to operate with the same level of authority.

This teaching has led to both men and women feeling the need to ensure that women stay in a place of worldly submission. Worldly submission wants you to stay in a subservient position. A place where your voice isn't important and you for sure do not have a place of influence. Worldly submission looks much like the proverb we've heard about women and children, that they "should be seen and not heard." Knowing what we have already read about Jesus, I would imagine that He is grieved by how we have applied Paul's words.

First, we need to note that several translations actually phrase this verse differently. That is because the word for man can also mean husband, and the word for woman can also mean wife. That is why in the English Standard Version it reads "the head of a wife is her husband," and in the New King James Version it says "the head of woman is man." The Greek word used in these verses for head is the word *kephalē*. For most of us, when we hear the word "head," we immediately think of the word "leader." It's a common word association in the English language. We can even use those words interchangeably at times, for instance, asking, "Who is the head of your department?" The problem with this word correlation is that it doesn't roll over into the Greek. In fact, the Greek lexicon shows that most of the translators did not regard "head" as the correct word to convey "leader."[8] A more probable understanding of the word *kephalē* is the word "source." So in light of that interpretation, these verses could be demonstrating that man came from Christ, woman came from man, and Christ comes from God.

Though this is a potential explanation for these two verses, we must still look at Ephesians to more deeply examine headship and address biblical submission. I don't ever want us to be in the habit of using a limited number of verses to defend our already firm theological positions. Instead, we want to study the whole of Scripture and formulate our theology from it.

Submit to one another out of reverence for Christ. Wives, submit yourselves to your own husbands as you do to the Lord. For the husband is the head of the wife as Christ is the head of the church, his body, of which he is the Savior. Now as the church submits to Christ, so also wives should submit to their husbands in everything. Husbands, love your wives, just as Christ loved the church and gave himself up for her to make her holy, cleansing her by the washing with water through the word, and to present her to himself as a radiant church, without stain or wrinkle or any other blemish, but holy and blameless. In this same way, husbands ought to love their wives as their own bodies. He who loves his wife loves himself. After all, no one ever hated their own body, but they feed and care for their body, just as Christ does the church—for we are members of his body. "For this reason a man will leave his father and mother and be united to his wife, and the two will become one flesh." This is a profound mystery—but I am talking about Christ and the church. However, each one of you also must love his wife as he loves himself, and the wife must respect her husband.

Ephesians 5:21–33 NIV

At first glance it feels as though Paul is trying to remind women that their main role is to submit, but one shocking point is important to note: Paul is supporting women in this chapter *simply by addressing them*! At that time, wives were of such low class culturally that they were not even worthy of being addressed, along with the other groups that Paul intentionally addresses in Ephesians 5, which are children and slaves.[9] At the time you only needed to address the one in authority because the others weren't considered of high enough value to be addressed. Paul is breaking the rules of ancient Middle Eastern culture by stating women, children, and slaves are all of value enough to be addressed in their own right.

In addition to this reality, we must also point out how Paul begins this instruction: "Submit to one another out of reverence for Christ" (v. 21). Hold up! This would have really taken aback the readers at the time. Paul is speaking to men, husbands, wives, women, children, and slaves, and he is telling them *all* to submit to *one another*. This cannot be taken as lightly as it is in our current culture. Under no circumstances in Paul's day would you have told husbands to submit to their wives, children, or especially their slaves. Paul is doing something extraordinary here if we can catch it. He is toppling the system that had been used to oppress many groups of people for generations. He is going right at the root of patriarchy, familial abuse, and slavery. I used to wonder why it appears—at face value—that Paul is okay with putting down women and supporting something as evil as slavery; however, when we understand the context, what we actually find is that Paul is brilliantly attacking those structures. He doesn't outright wear a T-shirt that says "I support women" or "Slavery is demonic"; instead, he comes alongside the culture and deals with the root of these issues. To a culture that is built on the oppression of others, Paul says, "Submit one to another out of reverence for Christ." If you want to honor Christ, then you must learn to submit one to another equally, not just one dominant group over a group of lesser value.

As Katia Adams points out, it is strange that in a chapter we have used to defend male leadership and authority, there's actually no mention of the words *leadership* and *authority*.[10] Paul doesn't say that wives should submit to their husbands and husbands should lead or exercise authority; instead, he says husbands should love. This passage, rather than trying to condone the domination of men over women, is actually attempting to liberate them from an oppressive system. Paul says that all of us should submit to one another, and yes, wives should submit to their husbands, just as the husbands should love their wives.

Some would ask the question, "Then why doesn't Paul directly instruct the men to submit?" It is an understandable question, but this does not imply that husbands aren't meant to submit to their wives. If that logic were followed, then we could ask the same question, "Why doesn't Paul instruct wives to love their husbands?" Is this to imply that if husbands are not meant to submit to their wives, then wives have no need to love their husbands? Of course not. That is a flawed interpretation and a weak attempt to justify oppression.

The truth is, Paul was bravely attacking the root of an oppressive culture. He was highlighting the value of wives, children, and slaves while encouraging those who had oppressed these groups to love them like Christ—not by asserting dominance, though their culture would allow this, but by demonstrating humility, submission, and kindness, as Jesus would do.

There are, of course, many other passages of Scripture we could go through and look at context, language, and other aspects to reveal that the Bible is not as oppressive toward women as we have been taught. I hope that in this chapter you can actually see that it is quite the opposite! Jesus and His Word support women. With great intention,

He chose to reveal the great value that women have to Him, even if our human culture does not hold women in that same regard. We should do the same.

I want us to be like Jesus. As women of God, followers of Christ, we must go out of our way to support each other. For too long the Bible has been used to limit women, when that was never Jesus' intention. If, like me, you can remember times when you felt the need to criticize women for "violating the Bible," then now is a really good time to broaden your perspective. The beauty is, it is not too late to change. Instead of putting other women down, using the Bible as a tool to hold them back, let's join together and support each other. That's what Jesus would do.

3

Managing Expectations

I'm not in this world to live up to your expectations and you're not in this world to live up to mine.

Bruce Lee

I'll be honest, I never thought we would live in a time when the question "What is a woman?" became some sort of a political statement. In a culture where even your gender is considered fluid, it is not shocking that more than ever we have identity issues permeating every level of society. As offensive as my next statement may be, I cannot move forward without making it: If you were born with a vagina, you are a woman, and most importantly, God made you a woman by design. It is not due to a random lottery or the luck of the draw that you are a woman; God wanted you to be a woman. There was no doubt a time in my life when that felt somewhat frustrating. I've already explained how I don't necessarily fit into the typical "woman stereotype."

This led many times to my wondering why God made me a woman, and if indeed it was intentional, what that meant for me. Why did I not fit into the typical mold? The more I have traveled and spoken to women, the more I've found that many of us have felt that way.

It isn't always, "Why did God make me a woman?" but it can be, "Why did He make me so out of the box and so unlike other women who seem somewhat normal?" Maybe you've thought, "Why does my heart feel so deeply and why do my emotions go from zero to ten so quickly?" I've spoken with many of you who wonder why you don't seem as passionate as other women, as fun as other women, as pretty—you can fill in the blank with the way you feel like you should be. The more I get to know you, the more I realize that you too share those identity questions that plagued me most of my life.

Our insecurities are inevitably exposed as we sit under the microscope of expectations. The *Barbie* movie brought a tidal wave of controversy regarding these issues when it was released, and although I do not approve of all its messages, one scene in the film resonated with me. As one of the characters hit her limit with the many expectations women deal with, she went on a rant that made me want to give a little charismatic praise dance and shout, "Amen!"

It is literally impossible to be a woman. You are so beautiful and so smart, and it kills me that you don't think you're good enough. Like, we have to always be extraordinary, but somehow we're always doing it wrong. You have to be thin, but not too thin. And you can never say you want to be thin. You have to say you want to be healthy, but also you have to be thin. You have to have money, but you can't ask for money because that's crass. You have to be a boss, but you can't be mean. You have to lead, but you can't squash other people's ideas. You're supposed to love being a mother, but don't talk about your kids all the . . . time. You have to be a career woman, but also always be looking out for other people. You have to answer for men's bad behavior, which is insane, but if you point that out, you're accused of complaining. You're supposed to stay pretty for men, but not so pretty that you tempt them too much or that you threaten other women because you're supposed to be a part of the sisterhood.[1]

Identity is meant to be found in Christ, as you no doubt know and have heard plenty of times; however, there is still the constant temptation to find our identity from outside sources. Taking this bait leads down a road that none of us wants to go on. If our value comes from someplace other than God, then we will likely do almost anything to make ourselves valuable. Unfortunately, this means we become vulnerable to the roller coaster of meeting everyone's expectations, and believe me, sister, it is a gnarly roller coaster of ups, downs, and wicked turns. To take the roller-coaster analogy maybe a little too far, this ride often leads us to vomiting all over ourselves and the women around us. This is a vicious cycle that I believe we can put a stop to by stepping back and getting a dose of perspective on expectations. When we as women feel we aren't meeting expectations, we can become vicious toward ourselves and each other.

We can avoid walking into this situation by addressing the expectations that make us feel insecure and lash out. The inability to meet expectations breeds insecurity and causes the formation of conflicted identity questions. We have many demands we're trying to meet just as friends, wives, or moms, and then we tack on what we've been told Jesus and the church expect from us. The expectations sitting on our shoulders cause us to question our identity and why we are the way we are. Meeting the expectations coming at us from a thousand different directions can feel impossible. These frustrations have led me to my knees countless times, crying out to God, "Why did you make me this way? Why can't I be more _____?" The struggle is real, girl, but as women we need to recognize we have a part to play that is bigger than just learning not to crush the women around us; we need to heal this issue in our own lives and the lives of the women around us.

Presumed Expectations

There are multiple types of expectations, and they are not all equal. The first kind we have to deal with is the expectations that we perceive and assume responsibility for when no one is actually putting them on us. Friend, to be vulnerable, this is one of the most frustrating areas for me. I call them presumed expectations. We work and work and serve and serve until we feel like we can't take it anymore. In desperation, we finally get the courage to tell our pastor, boss, friend, or spouse that we simply can't meet that expectation anymore.

If you're anything like me, at that point you secretly hope the person placing the "expectations" on you will acknowledge they are demanding too much. Public repentance would be nice, but I'll settle for private repentance—and then I am sure they will spread out those responsibilities that are causing me so much stress. This is my desired scenario; however, countless times the response I've received was simply, "I never asked you to do all that, so why don't you just stop doing so much?"

When I was young in ministry, I was on a staff of about ten people. We had weekly meetings to connect, discuss productivity, and go over what was being done and what needed to be done. Each week there were new tasks, and our boss would usually ask if anyone wanted to take them on. Every week I would raise my hand and add another task to my mounting list. I honestly thought the boss expected me to do so. Among the other members of the team, I had been in ministry the longest—and I was unmarried and thus didn't have the same number of family responsibilities, so my assumption was, "He expects me to do it; he's just giving me an option to be nice." On top of my assumption of his expectations, there was no doubt a large amount of my pride and overachieving nature that also assumed I could do it all, all the time.

This continued on week after week, with me raising my hand and putting more on my already full plate—until the plates shattered. I went to my boss, sat in his office, and cried. I began to apologize profusely for not meeting his expectations, for my weakness, for my inability to be what he needed me to be. I still cringe inside at his response. He said, "I've been waiting for this moment." I think my jaw might have dropped. He continued, "I knew there was no way you could keep up with all you were doing, but you were set on taking every task that was meant to be divided among the team. I was waiting for you to realize that you aren't Superwoman and you can't do it all."

Ugh. Ladies. Just *ugh*. Exposed. Utterly exposed, not because of the expectations he had of me, but because of the ones I assumed he did. In case you haven't realized it yet, you're not Superwoman, and neither am I. Don't get me wrong, you are capable of a lot, you are gifted, and you bring something unique to every environment you're in, but if you spend your life attempting to meet expectations that are actually not even there, you will never feel like you're "enough." This is a huge trap of the Enemy against us women, because when we feel insecure and less than, we often turn against each other.

We will address this more in another chapter, but if you're reading this, then I am willing to bet you have had this experience, whether you were the one who perpetrated it or it was done against you. Almost every woman has felt the sting of another insecure woman who turns on the women around her. This is one of the main reasons I'm writing this book. When we begin to see ourselves and others rightly, when we get healed, then we will stop turning on each other. It has to start here. No more sitting in a room, raising our hands to take on more than we can handle because we assume that's expected of us. No more turning our own insecurity onto other women and feeling like we have to compete with them to shine. Let's expose this demonic agenda right now. It is not always those around us who are heaping those expectations on us and urging us to do more. What if it's the Enemy? Paul informs us of the Enemy's deceptive tactics in 2 Corinthians 2:11 and warns us not to be unaware of his schemes. In his disgusting attempt to cause women to burn out and then turn on each other, the Enemy has no problem lying to us about what others expect of us.

Be on the lookout, ladies; you do not have to fall prey to his deceptive tactics.

Unrealistic Expectations

The second type of expectation is one I'm more willing to embrace. Some people just have unrealistic expectations of us. If we want to give them the benefit of the doubt, that's okay too, and we can say that it's not that they are demanding, but rather, we are in a season of life that makes those expectations not possible for us to meet. Maybe in a different season we could meet those expectations, but for whatever reason, in this one, we just can't.

Some people are incredibly demanding, but whichever viewpoint you want to take, the reality is you can't always meet everyone's expectations. Sister, do something for me right now. Take a deep breath. Breathe it all the way in and then breathe it all the way out. Now say with me, "I do not have to meet everyone's expectations." Okay, one more time for good measure: "I do not have to meet everyone's expectations." Raise your hand if you're also a recovering people pleaser. I have been there, way too many times. I want to be the best friend, daughter, believer, and minister that I can be, and many times that feels like constantly meeting the expectations of others. Unfortunately, it is not my sole duty in life to be what others want or even need me to be.

When I first started youth pastoring, I would sleep with my phone right next to my head. Listen, this was before anyone was talking about the effects of radiation from phones. I kept it there so that if any of the kids needed me, day or night, they could call me, and I would respond 100 percent of the time. So you can imagine my deep offense when a leader in my life once told me that not only did he not have to respond to my text messages when he was busy, but he also did not have to respond if he didn't want to. This was shocking. How in the world could a leader just decide not to respond to messages? That was downright ludicrous to me. It took me years to realize that in my naivety I felt that to be the most effective human I could be, I had to meet everyone's expectations.

Paul has some words to say about this in Galatians 1:10: "For am I now seeking the approval of man, or of God? Or am I trying to please man? If I were still trying to please man, I would not be a servant of Christ." Your fear of not meeting others' expectations can often keep you from becoming a true servants of Christ. The demands of man will keep you from walking in all that God has for you. Those expectations will keep you so busy toiling at things God never asked you to do that you will have no strength left for the things God has truly called you to do.

Someone once said, "If the devil can't make you sin, he'll make you busy." If someone is intentionally putting expectations on you, forgive them, love them, and then learn how to say an extremely powerful word: No. Dr. Henry Cloud says, "You only owe others what you have promised, not what they expect because it's what they want."[2] When you learn to give a really bold yes to what God has called you to do, then it becomes much easier to give a really strong no to what God is not telling you to do.

Unrealized Expectations

I am a big believer in spiritual parenting and discipleship. I work with young adults in a church culture that throws around titles like "spiritual mom" or "spiritual daughter" without really discussing what that means. Due to this setting I continuously have to deal with what I call unrealized expectations. These are expectations we have of others without necessarily consciously choosing to have them. This can be detrimental, especially when we use the word "mom" or "dad," because we all have our own loaded understandings of what to expect from a parent or even a parental figure. We don't sit down and thoroughly consider what those expectations are; we just expect them.

There isn't anything inherently wrong with having these expectations—unless we begin to implicate and judge the women we put those expectations on. I have been horribly guilty of this. As a young minister I was being discipled by a woman who deeply loved Jesus and loved me. We became so close that I began to call her Mom, because at the time I was learning a lot about having spiritual parents or mentors who were actively involved in your life. I still advocate that these relationships can be absolutely life-altering in the most positive way when we know how to do them in a godly and healthy manner; however, the closer we became, the more expectations I began to have of her. I never communicated these expectations because in actuality, I didn't realize that I had them. Since she had become a mother figure to me, I expected she would make time for me, tend to me, and care for me much in the way a mother would. It sounds really good, and quite possibly in a different season that could have worked out. But at this time she was pastoring, leading, and had a family of her own to take care of. The more she didn't meet my expectations, the more frustrated and critical of her I became. If we don't realize our expectations, then we can't communicate them, and if we cannot communicate them, then they certainly cannot be met or even addressed.

Thank God we can learn lessons from our mistakes. Now when I start to work with young women, whether it be in a professional setting or in a discipleship setting, I make it a point to have the "expectations" conversation. Most of the time I can tell they find this conversation to be highly unnecessary. It is difficult for us to state so bluntly what we want or even what we need, especially when we don't necessarily know what those expectations are until we think through them. But I force the young women I work with to think about and communicate what it is they expect. In this process of expectation discovery, they usually become aware of things about themselves as well. This is extremely important for us. We must be willing to take a candid look at ourselves and determine what we expect of those around us. If we ignore our unrealized expectations, they will inevitably turn outward toward other women.

Vocalizing Expectations

I have found that many of these scenarios can be avoided or at least clarified with one extremely honest conversation. I know we tend to hate these conversations, as they make us so vulnerable. I can still struggle in this area because I can quite naturally and frequently get in my head, and I don't want to make something big out of a circumstance that perhaps isn't as big as I feel it is; however, those types of assumptions can easily lead to a small situation becoming bigger than it ever needed to be.

I discovered the encouragement I needed to have these necessary clarifying conversations when I read Brené Brown's book *Dare to Lead*. I am not exaggerating when I say this book changed my life. It transformed how I lead and also just how I do relationships in general. In *Dare to Lead* Brené gives us this very simple, yet profound advice: "Clear is kind. Unclear is unkind."[3] She goes on to share about interviews she had with senior leaders in various environments, where she found one of the greatest concerns of these leaders was people avoiding tough conversations, including giving honest and productive feedback. Among a few different reasons for why we don't have those conversations was the fact that it is a cultural norm to be nice and polite. In other words, it is often seen as rude and impolite to have a direct and honest conversation. Yikes!

After years of making "clear is kind" a policy in my relationships and in the organizations I lead, I can tell you with certainty that being clear is incredibly kind and considerate. It is helpful to know what expectations people have of me and to communicate what expectations I have of others. I am no mind reader, and neither are you, though some of us women definitely teeter on the line of trying to be one. I might be able to cultivate a general idea of what is expected of me due to previous experience or my role in the situation, but at the end of the day I do not know what others expect of me until they communicate it.

If you need a certain level of one-on-one time, communication, alone time, support, encouragement, etc., then it is beneficial to let the other person know it. They cannot meet the expectations you have of them without communication that lets them know where the measuring tape even is.

So here is an important tip: Others don't know what you expect of them until you make it clear. It is not fair for me to expect a certain level of commitment or various tasks to be accomplished and never let my staff know my expectations. And this is a two-way street. They may have expectations of me—but I won't be able to meet them if I don't know they exist.

Making the effort to have this conversation can save hours or even years of wasted time and heartache. I encourage you to think of a few of those relationships or roles in which you feel like too much is expected of you. Once you've identified them, go to those involved and have a brave conversation. Ask them to clearly communicate exactly what is expected of you. This conversation will not always fix the problem of unrealistic expectations, but at least you now have the opportunity to converse about what is realistic and what you will or will not do.

Now let's do the really hard part. Take a minute and think about the expectations you have of others. Ask yourself: "What are the things I expect my girlfriends, coworkers, ministry leaders, etc., to do, but in actuality, I have never communicated to them?" If that stings a little bit, it's okay. We need to lean into that. Often we have hidden offense and bitterness toward others in our lives, and we have ruminated on their shortcomings and failures for far too long. We have sacrificed them on the altar of our unmet and perhaps unvocalized expectations. We have carried the pain of disappointment and rejection, not realizing that we never truly spoke out our needs. If that's you, there's grace, sis. Take the next couple of minutes and ask for God's forgiveness. Invite His grace to wash over your heart and help you to forgive the other person too if you need to. When it's the right timing, consider going to that person and sharing what God has shown you. You don't have to live with that junk anymore.

Finding God Expectations

The final scenario I'll look at is one that plagues us all. We just put ridiculous expectations on ourselves. It isn't that there are any perceived expectations or unrealistic expectations from another person; instead, all those heavy weights we're carrying were placed there by yours truly. The mental treadmill of thoughts that bombard us to do more and do it quicker seems to never stop. I wish that we could have a brave conversation with ourselves and clear up some of the confusion about what is truly expected. On our own, though, we won't be able to clear up all our confusion. The good news is, we can have a really brave conversation with God about it.

In my experience, when I go sit with God about the expectations I have of myself, almost always I find that I am being pushed by the Enemy instead of being led by Holy Spirit. Satan wants us to carry heavy burdens. He wants to convince us that we are never pleasing to our Father. The thoughts he throws at us contradict the nature of God and often send us into a tailspin of worry. If only we could be different, if only we could be better. The best way for God to be more satisfied with us is if we would do a lot more, a lot faster. John Mark Comer's book *The Ruthless Elimination of Hurry* is another treasure trove of valuable advice. In it he writes, "Love, joy, and peace are at the heart of all Jesus is trying to grow in the soil of your life. And all three are incompatible with hurry."[4] It makes sense that the driving urgency we often feel is not from God at all. In the realm of our own self-imposed expectations, it is imperative that we learn to discern the voice of God from the voice of the Enemy. God is not condemning, He is rarely in a rush (though He will let us know when something is urgent), and He is most definitely not withholding love from us based on our behavior.

When those intrusive thoughts of false expectations come, I say out loud so both the Enemy and my soul can hear me, "My Father doesn't sound like that!" I do not want to live under any expectations that God Himself hasn't set for me.

It is comforting to think that if we get rid of the unrealistic and false expectations, then all the pressures that lead to our insecurities will vanish; however, once we have rid ourselves of those, then we must face our very real responsibilities. We do not need to meet the heavy burdens we or others have placed on us, but if we don't show up for work on time, then we will likely get fired. If we stop feeding our kids or giving them the attention they need, then we might lose our spouse and the heart of our family. Not all expectations placed on us are bad; many of them are very real responsibilities that we chose when we said yes to other things. Saying yes to a spouse, kids, a job, or a ministry—all of those yeses come with responsibility, and I would go so far as to say they are God-ordained responsibilities.

In addition to discerning His voice from the voice of the accuser, it is extremely helpful to learn practical and valuable skills in the self-management of our lives. Let us not, by lack of discipline, produce unnecessary crises and challenges. Learning to apply discipline and organization in the overarching pursuit of my roles, both in relationships and in ministry, has had a profound impact on overcoming my insecurities, and subsequently on healing any form of identity issues. I struggle less with the confronting thoughts of accusation when I am taking the time to hear God's voice, as well as managing myself and my time well.

One invaluable tool when considering expectations and responsibilities is called the Eisenhower Matrix. In short, the matrix is a task management tool that helps us acknowledge what tasks deserve priority in our day-to-day lives. The matrix is based off a quote from President Dwight D. Eisenhower in a 1954 speech when he said, "I have two kinds of problems, the urgent and the important. The urgent are not important, and the important are never urgent." Stephen Covey, the author of *The 7 Habits of Highly Effective People*, took Eisenhower's words and created the matrix, also called the Urgent-Important Matrix.

	Urgent	Not Urgent
Important	Visit friend in hospital. Pay bills. Have group call for board meeting. Write notes for service.	Plan meeting for retreat. Respond to emails/texts. Write notes for upcoming conference. Do laundry.
Not Important	Pack for itinerant trip. Go grocery shopping.	Have coffee with a friend. Paint bathroom. Buy chair for living room. Brainstorm for next book.

As you can see, the matrix has four quadrants, which divide tasks up into four categories: urgent and important, urgent and not important, not urgent and important, and not urgent and not important. The matrix helps you to establish which of your responsibilities and expectations should take precedence in your life. The more you can identify which quadrant your tasks are in, the more you can make decisions from the healthy place of focusing on the responsibilities God has given you and fewer of the unnecessary expectations placed on you. The matrix even gives solutions for what to do with tasks that fall into specific quadrants. For instance, if a task is urgent but not important, then that task can be delegated. Many times a task might be important to someone else, but unimportant to you in light of what God has asked of you. That is the perfect time to delegate that task to someone else who finds it important or has the ability to do it without maxing out their capacity.

This might feel way too elementary and practical for you, but when applied, I have found that it works wonders for women who have struggled with certain insecurities. It turns out that we all feel a lot better about our roles when we eliminate unnecessary tasks and expectations.

Sister, you can take off the weight of expectations that are on your shoulders and step into the yoke of Jesus. His yoke is easy, and His burden is light (Matthew 11:30). You absolutely can stop putting false expectations on yourself and on those around you. On the other side is freedom. When you fully let go of the superfluous expectations, then you can wholeheartedly embrace your God-given responsibilities and purpose.

This is where the secret sauce is. It is your golden spot. This is the place where the anointing of God meets your God-given design. Here is where identity issues are obliterated. Girl, there is nothing like that place of grace where you know that you know you're in the right place, the right relationship, the right role, at the right time. Not everyone else may be pleased with you, but you are confident in His pleasure with you. Your footsteps are lighter because you aren't carrying the baggage of needing the approval of man, and you aren't listening to the condemning words of the Enemy. We charismatics would say that you have "entered in"! You are in the space God designed for you.

One of the consequential benefits of this revelation is that it allows us to celebrate others around us joyfully. As women we can look at other women and compassionately help them to break out of the expectations that are so common among us. I want to support women so they don't succumb to the insecurities that come from always trying to meet these chaotic expectations around us. I do not want one single woman around me to suffer under the weight of an identity crisis caused by misplaced expectations.

My friend, I want you to thrive in the contentment of being fully confident that you are fearfully and wonderfully made. God has specifically designed you with purpose. You don't need to meet any expectations that He hasn't specifically given you.

4

Our Greatest Enemy

Don't give the enemy a seat at your table.

Louie Giglio, *Don't Give the Enemy
a Seat at Your Table*

Over the course of the research for this book, I have heard countless, albeit appalling, stories from women about the damage they have incurred from other women in their lives. As we continue through this book together, you'll hear some of these stories and likely be reminded of your own as we address head-on the issues that display some of the worst aspects of our gender; however, we need to remember that these women are not our enemies.

I was at coffee with a friend, and as we sipped our steaming cups of flavorful heaven, we discussed a situation where another person had essentially gone off the rails. This person's behavior had become erratic, uncharacteristic, and as my grandma used to say at times, "just downright hateful." As my friend looked me in the eyes searching for some shred of wisdom, "Well, that is just demonic" came flying out of my mouth before I had the chance to consider my words. We sat in silence for a moment as she soaked in the reality that I'd unintentionally blurted out, and I contemplated whether this was a truth from Holy Spirit or just another time that my filter didn't do its best filtering.

The Bible tells us that "we do not wrestle against flesh and blood, but against principalities, against powers, against the rulers of the darkness of this age" (Ephesians 6:12 NKJV). In the midst of our emotions blowing up like firecrackers on the Fourth of July, it can be difficult to remember this truth. Like in so many things, we see the physical person standing in front of us, and we don't see the spiritual force that might be working right below the surface. We see this demonstrated in what I find to be one of the more comical scenes of the Bible, as Jesus boldly confronts Peter in Mark 8:33 (NIV): "But when Jesus turned and looked at his disciples, he rebuked Peter. 'Get behind me, Satan!' he said. 'You do not have in mind the concerns of God, but merely human concerns.'"

When I read passages in the Bible, I like to put myself into them, really imagine what the atmosphere would be like in the moment and how the people in the story would have felt. This is one of those stories that gives me a chuckle, as I can imagine how humbled Peter must have felt. Our dear Peter is devoted, and that's understating it a bit. He has left everything to follow Jesus, and his zeal is a straight-up eleven out of ten. How could it not be? Jesus found him as a simple fisherman and transformed his life into something great. He became one of the Messiah's closest friends and a leader who himself would lay hands on the sick and see them recover. Peter was growing in authority and learning to live the ways of the kingdom. He was excelling in the Jesus school of ministry program. Unfortunately, Peter wasn't just gifted and anointed; he was also prideful, with a little side effect that I know all too well: the astonishing ability to be extremely quick to speak and slow to listen.

In Mark 8, Peter is first praised for recognizing Jesus as the Messiah, and just four short verses later he is being rebuked. What could have possibly transpired for ol' Pete to go from declaring Jesus as Messiah to literally having his friend and leader so directly rebuke him? Well, Jesus was explaining to His disciples that He would indeed have to suffer, be rejected, and even be killed. He plainly assured them that He would rise again in three days, but Peter wasn't having any of this suffering and death talk. Honestly, I can't blame him. I probably wouldn't have clapped for that message either. I mean, come on, Peter was the one who had correctly identified Jesus as Messiah—he has some "street cred" here—so our bold Peter decided he would just pull aside the Son of God and give Him a good talking-to. I don't know if I find this so funny because it sounds that incredibly ludicrous to me or because down in the crevices of my heart, I can see myself doing the same thing. Sometimes it stings less if you laugh about it.

After Peter's rebukes, we find the verse in which Jesus says to Peter, "Get behind me, Satan! . . . You do not have in mind the concerns of God, but merely human concerns" (Mark 8:33 NIV). I've heard some preachers suggest that Jesus was actually talking to the spirit at work through Peter in that moment. Whether Jesus was calling Peter himself Satan or addressing the demonic spirit at work through him, the implication is the same. Peter's rebuke of Jesus wasn't coming from the fruit of the Spirit or even from himself; it was demonically instigated. I think it's helpful to note that Jesus didn't bother with addressing Peter's intentions in the moment; instead, He went full-force against the source behind it.

The Source behind the Attack

Many times, if not most of the time, we don't take the time to recognize the source behind our attack. It might appear to come through our friend, our mother, our coworker, or our leader, but the source is not that woman; it is actually demonic. This passage is refreshing to me because it helps me realize that even the most loyal followers of Jesus can be manipulated by the Enemy. The most shocking realization, however, is that this is not Peter's worst betrayal story, though that will come soon. This is immediately following one of Peter's success stories. This is in his "I'm really crushing it as a follower of Jesus" phase.

We have all wondered how in the world it is possible that a woman we look up to could possibly "act like that" or "say those harsh things." I have sat in my room crying, asking God how it could be possible that a fellow sister in Christ could be so cruel. I know there are Cruella de Vils and Mean Girls out there, but honestly, I never expected that once I became a believer we would continue to treat each other in such an un-Christlike manner. These few little verses give us some insight. That nasty Enemy can lie to us not just when we are running away from God, but even right after we were so clearly in tune with Holy Spirit.

This realization produces some relief in my heart for the moments when I was the one who hurt someone, and it should produce some grace for the times when someone has hurt me. We have all been on both sides of the equation, the villain and the victim.

Recognizing the Accuser

As much as I would love to believe, like Peter, that once I've reached a proverbial distinct level of maturity I will no longer hear or believe the lies of the Enemy, we all know that isn't true. The disgusting tactics of Satan know no age boundaries.

Several years ago a girl named Ashley (not her real name) moved to town to attend the church and ministry school I was involved with. Ashley was talented and had a lot of favor on her life. It seemed like she was getting some new recognition or promotion every few months. As Ashley appeared to excel professionally, privately I began to hear stories about her that were less than commendable. These accusations were about Ashley's attitude, work ethic, even her morality or Christlikeness. Although I had never spent any significant time with Ashley, I began to avoid her altogether, not wanting to "deal with" a person of her character. I reasoned within myself that Ashley was definitely not the type of person I wanted in my circle of friends. I had made that judgment entirely based on the whispers I'd heard behind closed doors.

Eventually our worlds collided, and I was quite literally forced to work alongside Ashley. What I found was astounding. Ashley was an extremely hard worker, with an incredibly positive attitude and even more impeccable character. In a later chapter we'll discuss the jealous spirit that most likely fueled the lies spoken about Ashley, but what I learned was that the lies the Enemy tells us about ourselves and about other women can potentially derail a God-given relationship or purpose. Ashley and I went on to become great friends, and we are still close today. Ours is a friendship that was almost completely missed because of lies.

Without a doubt, the lies the Enemy tells us and other women cause incalculable amounts of unnecessary division, pain, and offense. This chapter is not meant to bring any type of glory to the Enemy or to instill fear in you, but rather to expose the works of the Enemy (Ephesians 5:11). Paul also tells us that he does not want us to be ignorant of the schemes of the Enemy (2 Corinthians 2:11). All too often, we fall into one of two camps regarding Satan: We either see him behind every corner, blaming the Enemy for even our slightest inconveniences (who hasn't spilled their coffee and wondered why Satan hates them so much?), or we completely ignore his existence and fail to recognize when he's at work. Neither of these positions is beneficial for our walk with Christ or our relationships with each other. We must recognize the Enemy's schemes while acknowledging that "greater is he that is in [us], than he that is in the world" (1 John 4:4 KJV).

When we learn to identify the lies the Enemy is using against us, then we can prevent various relational tensions and obstacles that come from believing those lies. Pastor Bill Johnson says, "When we believe a lie, we empower the liar."[1] Fortunately the opposite is true as well: When we believe the truth, we believe the Truth Maker. As godly women we need to make every effort to seek the truth and disregard the lies. It is truth that sets us free, and it is lies that leave us in bondage. That bondage produces offense and division among women.

We do not have enough space in this book to cover every type of lie the Enemy will try to use against us, but I do want to identify three common lies I have seen in my life and in the lives in my community. The Enemy uses these lies to manipulate our behavior toward other women and destroy God-ordained purposes. My prayer is that as you read this, you will become aware of how the Enemy has manipulated you and your relationships with other women so that we can kick him out of our lives and our relationships once and for all.

Lies about Another's Motives

One of the most common types of lies are the ones that cause us to question another woman's motives. Oh, girl. If we were able to sit down to a nice big cup of coffee and chat, I am certain you could tell me stories of when other women questioned your motives. This lie manifests in an accusatory and prideful tone that assumes we can easily know the intention of another woman's heart.

I remember the time a friend confronted me because she hadn't been invited to a movie outing with a few of our girlfriends. The friend who wasn't invited had created an entire story in her head that we were all rejecting her and no longer wanted to be her friend. The Enemy was running amok in her mind with accusations about our motives. What she didn't know was that I knew her husband was planning to take her out on a surprise date that night, so I wanted to spare her making plans with us, buying movie tickets, and then having to cancel. Where she thought our hearts were against her, they were actually for her, but the Enemy was lying to her about our motivations.

The Enemy's voice will sound something like this: "They did that just to hurt you!" Goodness, it stinks so much when you find out the person you judged wasn't trying to hurt you. Maybe she was having a bad day, maybe she'd been in a fight with her spouse, or perhaps what you took so personally was in reality not about you at all.

As a speaker I have had to have conversations about my motives many times. Let me first state that I don't mind these conversations. I by far prefer another woman to come and ask me a direct question rather than assume they know my motives; however, I have lost count of how many times in a service or conference I have accidentally walked by a friend or acquaintance and didn't stop to acknowledge them. The narrative the Enemy tells them is "Jessika doesn't like you" or "She is offended by you" or any other accusatory lie he can use to make them think I purposely ignored them.

If I have done that to you, let me apologize first, and then explain that I move with purpose. What that means is that in church settings I can be so focused on whatever the next thing I am doing is that I do a terrible job of recognizing all my friends around me. This isn't necessarily a valid excuse for the behavior, but it is certainly not intentional or malicious. The glaring problem with lies of judging another's motives is crystal clear: We do not always see the full picture. Now, I know that not everyone's motives are always pure. The Bible also warns us to be "wise as serpents and innocent as doves" (Matthew 10:16).

Recommendation: We will address more in a later chapter how to deal with women who purposely hurt you and cause division, but for now, let me provide a suggestion on what to do every time you assume a woman's motives are ill-natured: Take it before the Father. God alone is omniscient. He can see far beyond surface-level interactions. He sees the context, the past, and the future. We see in part; He sees it all, and that's why we should trust Him more than we trust ourselves. Bring that female and that situation before Him, and ask Him to give you His heart for that person and that situation. You will be shocked by His perspective.

Lies of Comparison

Another common type of lie is the lie of comparison. This lie can take so many different forms, ranging anywhere on the spectrum from believing that someone is better than you to believing that you are better than them. This type of lie plays on our pride and insecurities, leading us to judge someone, often on face value. I'm slightly embarrassed to admit it, but this type of lie used to plague me almost daily. I would walk into the rec center at my university and immediately notice every other woman's body size in the room, making immediate comparisons between their body type and mine. If I walked into a workout class and there were mostly women who looked stronger or in better shape than me, I would immediately become insecure and want to leave. The lie of comparison tried to tell me what rooms I was allowed to be in and which ones I wasn't.

As I grew older, the filthy thoughts of comparison followed me into ministry. I would listen to other women preach and compare myself to them. If I felt they were more gifted than me, I would become insecure, and if I didn't think they were as good as me, I would feel confident that I could impress the crowd. What a nasty spirit comparison is. I've even seen this at work in my close friendships with other women. Several years ago I had a friend who seemed to have the perfect life. I assumed her husband always did the dishes and her kids always respectfully used "Yes, ma'am." She was being promoted in her job, so naturally I believed her bank account must be bursting at its seams. Apparently, she was the one person in the world who just never had any challenges. And that felt so unfair. The more I ruminated on the lies of comparison I was believing, the more I felt the urge to pull further away from the friendship. Division was occurring, until one day we sat down and had a heart-to-heart. Little did I know that she felt the same way about me. In her eyes I didn't have a spouse or family to take care of, I had a substantial amount of free time, I traveled whenever I wanted, and I clearly spent every day reveling in my extravagant freedom.

No one ever wins in the game of comparison. If you appear in your eyes as better off, then you will step into pride, and if you see yourself as less than, then you will slide into insecurity. The Enemy wants you to play the comparison game. I heard someone once say, "Comparison is a thief of joy!" It is impossible to live your life believing the lies of comparison and live in the joy, unity, and fulfillment of the Lord.

I recently did a poll for women on my Instagram story. I asked women what they believed were the biggest lies the Enemy told women about other women. Over half of the responses involved some form of comparison. One of the most enlightening insights I discovered from these comments was that after lies of comparison usually came some form of rejection. When we compare ourselves to other women, we will reject that woman or assume they are rejecting us. I was shocked to find that comparison was so closely accompanied by rejection. The two work in tandem with each other.

Women have told me repetitively that the lie they most often believe is that some woman is better than they are and thus would never want to be friends with them. Long before they have ever had the chance to meet or spend time together, the lie of comparison has caused rejection to have its way. Partnering with the lies of comparison is truly like rearranging the deckchairs on the *Titanic*. Not only is it a waste of your time, but it will also lead to you being stuck in a sinking boat.

Recommendation: The best way to combat lies of comparison is to fully embrace your God-given uniqueness and identity. You will not always be the most beautiful, fit, talented, anointed, wealthy woman in the room, and you for certain will not always be the least in the room, but honestly, in the end who cares anyway? You are who God made you to be, and that is what is most important. To quote the famous Dr. Seuss, "Today you are you, that is truer than true. There is no one alive who is youer than you!"[2] God made you unique, and no one else can do you like you can. If you won't step into the fullness of who God created you to be, then the world will miss out on the expression of God that He intended to come through you. When we as women become confident in our identity in Christ, then we expose the lies of comparison that hinder our unity.

Lies of Mistrust

This category of lies can cross over with the category of lies about another's motives, but this type of lie is so common and so damaging I knew it needed to be addressed in its own category. There is a gender stereotype that women are willing to lie, gossip, and betray each other for personal gain. This has led to collective mistrust of other women in a vast array of areas. We instinctively believe other women are after our man, will tell our secrets, or are deviously plotting our demise. I have watched lies of mistrust ruin the closest of friendships and sabotage the potential of kingdom-building partnerships.

As a single female in ministry I have unfortunately been on the losing end of this type of lie more times than I can even count. The fact is that in my line of work I am in the minority, and I find myself surrounded by men in conference greenrooms, strategy meetings, and other work-related settings. This is a reality I am determined to see rectified in my lifetime, with women consistently having a seat at the table, but for now it is the situation I find myself in.

Due to this repeating scenario, I've had to have multiple conversations with fellow women to assure them that I am not the least bit interested in their spouses. Simply by my being in the same room with a group of people, the Enemy has lied and tried to make the other woman feel like I was interested in her husband. For this very reason I have chosen to go out of my way to avoid sitting with or conversing overly much with men whose spouse I don't have a previous relationship with.

I do not mind doing my part to make another woman feel safe when her husband is out doing itinerate ministry; in fact, I think this is one incredible way that we can support the women who stay at home to raise a family while their husband goes out to minister. However, it is quite discouraging and painful to find out that another woman assumes the worst about me with no basis except the fact that I am a single female. I can tell you from personal experience, those lies of mistrust run deep, especially when it comes to the men in our lives, whether it be our spouses, boyfriends, or even just platonic friendships. Hell hath no fury like a woman who thinks another woman is hitting on her man.

I fervently believe that as women we should go above and beyond in protecting marriages and relationships by not allowing even a hint of dishonorable behavior. We should willingly and gladly go to the extreme in protecting the trust of other women, especially in regard to their husbands. Simultaneously, the Enemy knows that one of the quickest ways to destroy a relationship between women is to cause mistrust, so he will tell us that we cannot trust another woman, often through unsubstantiated claims.

Obviously, it is not just with our men that these lies attack us. My friend Abby, bless her sweet soul, is a strong, independent woman. When we first met, our friendship just clicked. I noticed over time that though Abby was a blast to spend time with, she would circumvent personal questions and even leave the room at times when our friends would start having a heart-to-heart. After a few months I finally addressed the questions that had been rolling around in my head from the beginning. Why did it appear that Abby completely avoided a deeper connection with us? Without hesitation Abby confessed that she simply did not trust women. Upon further discovery, I learned that Abby had been told by her mother for years growing up that women will take what is said to them, no matter how personal it might be, twist it around, then repeat it to others. For Abby's entire life she had believed that no women were worthy of trust, and thus she had missed numerous opportunities for meaningful friendships with other women. I can't help but wonder how many of you reading this book have been told and believed similar lies. I hate to think how many incredible relationships we've missed out on because of the Enemy's stupid lies.

Many of the lies the Enemy throws at us are able to take root in us because they capitalize on pride in our lives. A lie is whispered in our ear assuming someone's motives, and our pride says, "Yes! You have great discernment; you know exactly what she was thinking, feeling, doing, wanting when she said or did that!" It is our pride that comes into agreement with comparison, convincing us that we are a good enough judge to measure ourselves up against our sisters. Pride again will have us believing that we may be trustworthy, but surely no other woman is. That same pride that allows us to make judgments against our sisters will encourage us to spread our judgments with others, repeating the cycles that created this mess in the first place.

For years I have been deeply convicted by a set of verses where Jesus models for us a better response:

> For to this you have been called, because Christ also suf-
> fered for you, leaving you an example, so that you might
> follow in his steps. He committed no sin, neither was
> deceit found in his mouth. When he was reviled, he did
> not revile in return; when he suffered, he did not threaten,
> but continued entrusting himself to him who judges justly.
>
> 1 Peter 2:21–23

Though He had never sinned, He still faced suffering and reviling at the hands of man. In return He did not judge, threaten, gossip, slander, or any of our choice methods; instead, the Word says that He entrusted himself to Him who judges justly. Jesus, the Son of God, decided to allow the Father to be the just judge. Jesus also tells us in John 7:24, "Do not judge by appearances, but judge with right judgment." God is the most just judge, and many times the bait of the Enemy's lies convinces us to step into the place of judge and pronounce judgment on situations and other women when we have no right to. When we choose to step in and be the judge, we rob ourselves of the opportunity of having God not only be the judge but be our defense. I don't know about you, but I would much rather have God defend me than have to defend myself. He is a really good judge and a really good defender. I would much rather hear His truth about the women around me than believe the lies the Enemy is trying to convince me of. Despite the numerous lies the Enemy has told us about women, I have found that far too often we have just been duped, and actually women are freaking incredible. It is from other women that I have found the encouragement to embrace the call of God on my life, it is from other women that I have found close-knit sisters, and it is through other women that I have been challenged to draw even nearer to Christ.

We have too much to lose by empowering the Enemy in our lives. You and I have lost enough. Let's work together with our sisters in Christ and do as Jesus did: destroy the works of the Enemy (1 John 3:8) by exposing the lies he tells us. Together we can resist the devil and watch him flee (James 4:7) by taking every thought captive and putting it into obedience to Christ (2 Corinthians 10:5). When you and I refuse to believe the Enemy's lies about other women, we can begin to see the true unity among women that God desires for us. The more I have researched for this book, the more convinced I am that God truly has a unique plan for women in this hour if we are willing to stop taking the bait of Satan and choose sisterhood. So it is time—right now, as you're reading this book—to make the decision to link arms and run with our sisters in Christ!

5

Destroying Jealousy and Competition

The day you look at other women and celebrate their strengths instead of think of them as competition is the day you go from a girl to a woman.

Alli Worthington

It is impossible for jealousy and a healthy relationship to coexist. Think about that for a second. Any time jealousy enters a relationship, it will begin to bleed its poison into every aspect of our thinking and decision-making. Too often we let jealousy run rampant in our hearts to the point that we lash out, even using any means necessary to sabotage our fellow women. Let me just level with you, that type of behavior is not shocking at all from our unsaved neighbors, but it is appalling from those who call themselves disciples of Christ. And yet, as you and I both know, it is far too common. It is a sin that we tend to accept as normal, especially among women.

The process of writing this book and interviewing other women on this topic opened my eyes in a whole new way to just how widespread jealousy is among us. I am certainly not writing this from an ivory tower as someone who has never dealt with jealousy myself, but I am insisting that as Christians, this is not a heart issue we should tolerate or be dismissive about in ourselves or our communities.

The book of James has pretty direct words for us on the topic:

> But if you have bitter jealousy and selfish ambition in your hearts, do not boast and be false to the truth. This is not the wisdom that comes down from above, but is earthly, unspiritual, demonic. For where jealousy and selfish ambition exist, there will be disorder and every vile practice. But the wisdom from above is first pure, then peaceable, gentle, open to reason, full of mercy and good fruits, impartial and sincere.
>
> James 3:14–17

If you've ever wondered where jealousy stems from, you can trace it all the way back to the original sin of Lucifer's pride. Everything Satan did to rebel against God was coupled with jealousy. He wanted what God had. He uses the same root of jealousy to manipulate us today. According to Cyprian of Carthage, to be jealous is to imitate the devil.[1]

Cyprian leaves no room for misinterpretation as he echoes James. Both are clarifying that jealousy and even selfish ambition are not to be confused with being loving, cute, or ambitious; instead, they are labeled as demonic. At its root, jealousy is not just an offense against my sister; it's a sin against God. When I choose to be jealous of someone else for their talents, possessions, circumstances, etc., I am telling God that what He has given me is not enough, that I need more. Over time jealousy corrupts how we see others, including those whom we once called friend. It brings toxicity into our behavior, causing us to treat other women in irrational ways.

When I think of how jealousy weasels its way into our relationships, I think of the famous book-turned-movie *Little Women*. One particularly iconic exchange gives dramatic imagery to the reality of just how petty jealousy can be. If you've read the book or seen the movie, I am sure you remember this scene well. Amy is extremely upset with her sister Jo for not letting her join her and her friends for a night out at the theater. In her fit of jealousy over Jo getting to go while she didn't, Amy takes her sister's manuscript, which is Jo's most prized possession, and throws it into the fire, completely destroying it. Countless females over the years have watched this scene in shock (and occasional humor) as jealousy over one simple thing leads Amy into destructive revenge. After discovering what Amy has done, Jo confronts her, and Amy yells, "I told you I'd make you pay for being so cross yesterday, and I have."[2]

We must either drop our jaw in awe or laugh hysterically at the absurdity of Amy's behavior. These two sisters who actually love each other deeply both experience the pain of jealousy's brutal demands. Although Amy's behavior is somewhat comical to us when we watch the movie, I can't help but think how many times jealousy has made me or someone I know act out immaturely as well. In real life it just isn't that becoming of an adult woman to behave in such a juvenile manner.

In our lives, we may not be burning each other's books—thankfully no one got their hands on this one—but we still allow jealousy to influence us in the most nonsensical ways. If we are brutally honest with ourselves, we realize that jealousy leads us to be immature and ungodly, causing us to eventually be ashamed of our actions. Even Amy in *Little Women* deeply regretted burning the book after she calmed down.

Jealousy will either try to force you to ruin your relationship with other women by acting out in a destructive manner, or possibly even cause you to pull away from women you feel jealous toward. I've seen women distance themselves when their friends began to make more money or became famous. It's as if they couldn't tolerate being around their friend anymore simply because of their success. Week over week they slowly removed themselves from the friendship. Many times jealousy is way more subtle than it was with Amy. Jealousy may not cause a major burn-the-book, knock-'em-out fight, but it always refuses to let you just have a healthy relationship. We have to be on the lookout for evidence of jealousy in our hearts and in our relationships.

Not long ago I was taking a few minutes to scroll through my Instagram feed, and I saw a sweet friend of mine post about a recent success in her life. As soon as I saw the post, my heart sank a little. I swiped out of the app and just sat with this gross, negative feeling in the pit of my stomach. I stopped and took a moment to ask Holy Spirit what was going on in my heart. I knew I "should" feel happy for my friend, so why didn't I? As I asked Him for direction, He brought that correction we all so desperately need: "Jessika, you're jealous because you don't think I will do that for you."

Cue another one of those humbling, make-you-want-to-cry moments. I knew right then and there that I didn't want that nasty jealousy to work its way any deeper into my heart. I truly wanted to celebrate my friend's victories, or at least I wanted to want to celebrate my friend's victories! I repented to Him and admitted that I did indeed question whether or not He would do the same for me. That doubt in my heart made me jealous that He would do it for her. As I said earlier, jealousy tells God that what we have is not enough. If we really want to get to the nitty-gritty of it, then jealousy is revealing an area where I lack trust and faith. I don't trust God to know what's best for me, or I don't have the faith to believe He'll do it for me too.

I wasn't jealous because I didn't love my friend. I wasn't even jealous because I didn't want her to have that blessing. I was jealous because when I saw what she had, it revealed insecurity and doubt in my own heart. I had two choices when Holy Spirit revealed what was happening: I could dismiss it as normal or I could repent. Far too often we dismiss these little issues in our hearts, and that's where the trouble starts. Then, as jealousy grows, it breeds those unholy actions women tend to be known for. This does not have to be our normal.

Friend, you can stop being jealous of other women. You can stop those thoughts from the Enemy right in their tracks. You do not have to entertain thoughts of jealousy. How wonderful it would be if we saw other women that were beautiful, talented, and successful, and instead of being jealous we felt excited for them. How truly honoring of God and each other would it be if instead of being tempted to criticize, gossip, or sabotage, we wanted to celebrate and bless them.

As women we need to make war against jealousy. We should not tolerate jealousy sabotaging us any longer. What if women weren't known for their jealousy of each other, but instead for their support for each other?

The Cure for Jealousy

The cure for jealousy is practiced gratefulness. When you are grateful for what has been given to you, then you no longer need to be jealous of what has been given to another. The best way to shut up the lies of jealousy is to begin to speak the truth of gratefulness. You may not have the house she has, maybe you didn't get the promotion she got, or maybe you haven't yet found your husband like she just did, but I can promise you that God has done much for you. He is a faithful God, and He knows how to father each of His daughters exactly how they need to be parented. You might not have all the things that she has or be all the things she is, though you do have all the things God has given you and you are who God has made you to be.

As Bill Johnson says, "Anyone who knows who God made them to be will never try to be someone else."[3] When we become grateful for who God has made us to be and what He has given to us, then the Enemy's attempts to fill us with jealousy are destroyed. The next time you notice jealousy trying to creep in, I encourage you to refuse it and choose gratefulness instead.

Jealousy and Competition

Jealousy and competition often go hand in hand. If you show me a jealous person, I am willing to bet they're also competitive with other women. I heard a story from a woman named Abby who shared how she had been affected by competition among women. She had lived in a house with other single women her age, and they had all been great friends—until Mr. Dreamy entered from stage right.

One of the roommates, Sonia, had met this new guy named Adam, and she was instantly attracted to him, as was apparently every girl in church within a fifty-mile radius. He was attractive, he was successful, he loved Jesus, and most importantly, he was single. Abby, of course, noticed how good-looking he was when she first met him but knew Sonia had feelings for him. She decided the best thing she could do was be nice to him and try to give him a little nudge in Sonia's direction.

However, when Veronica, their other roommate, met Adam, she immediately began flirting with him. After all, there was only a limited number of men like Adam to go around. It was less than a week before Sonia became extremely jealous and angry. Before you knew it, both Veronica and Sonia were criticizing each other in front of Adam. Every flaw that could be pointed out publicly was being aired like dirty laundry.

The longer this went on the more demeaning it became, at times resorting to questionable truths being shared. In the end Sonia threw Abby into the boxing match as well. Depending on the time of day, Abby was accused of flirting with Adam too, or not being a good friend for not

89

gossiping and rejecting Sonia. The competition was in full force, and apparently everyone needed to take a side. This is the problem with treating kingdom relationships like sporting matches. There isn't a "my team" and "her team." Under the blood of Jesus, we're all on the same team.

In less than two months the friendships were all destroyed, the girls had to find new homes, and Adam began dating another girl outside of their friend group. Hearing the story made me feel like I was listening to *Othello*: All hope is lost, and everything just blows up in the end. How discouraging.

I was raised in a highly competitive family. I remember tackling my brother on the concrete basketball court simply because he was beating me in a pickup game of one-on-one. I had a pretty consistent and ignorant motto when it came to certain competitions: "If you can't beat 'em, injure 'em." As ludicrous as this sounds to me now as an adult, it appears to be how women think it works in life. We compete for our desired outcome, and if we don't think we can win, we get nasty.

As a coach I used to tell people I would have no problem breaking up a fight between two males, but I would never try to stop a fight between two females. The moment I stepped in between men, they would break apart and go their separate ways; however, the women would just drag me down to the ground with them while their nails kept scratching anything that got in their way.

Thankfully, most of you are likely not the type to start pulling out earrings and throwing punches. You may not become physically violent like I was with my brother or even choose any form of direct aggression toward another woman, but many women will resort to indirect aggression instead. Indirect aggression is the way we attack other women without facing them head on. It looks like starting rumors about another woman in order to distort how other people view her. It can look like ostracizing a woman we feel threatened by. A friend of mine once told me that when her now-husband first started showing interest in her, several women in her church went to him and subtly gave reasons for why she wasn't dateable. That is definitely indirect aggression. The list can go on and on of all the creative ways we can think of to hurt or sabotage a woman who feels like competition to us.

Competition is a problem that unfortunately even affects ministry circles. I've acknowledged the disheartening reality that many times there really isn't as much opportunity for women inside the church as there is for men, and I know many women feel the same way in corporate settings outside the church as well. This perceived or actual lack is known as resource scarcity, and it has led to the feeling that we need to compete for our place instead of choosing to trust the Lord with our journey. If we are convinced there is a limit of resources, promotions, opportunities, or even men, then we begin to fight each other to try to get what we need or want.

Unfortunately, I have seen this in some of the most devastating circumstances around the world in countries of extreme poverty. When people haven't eaten in a long time, they are overwhelmed by a carnal instinct to do whatever is necessary to get the food they so desperately need. We often refer to this condition as the "orphan spirit." It describes the way we behave when we forget that we have a good Father who takes care of us. When we forget that, we can become the worst versions of ourselves in our attempt to make a way for ourselves.

I remember counseling a young woman who came to me asking for advice one time when her ex-boyfriend began to date another woman. This normally cheerful and kind young woman was saying such hostile, rude comments about the girl who was dating her ex. She was so jealous and sad upon hearing the news that she began to lash out. I am sure most of us can relate to that feeling at one point in life or another. After seeing how upset she was, I asked her a pretty simple question: "Do you still want to be with him?" Her answer made me laugh, as she was adamant that she had no good feelings toward him and didn't want to be with him at all. "So . . . you're telling me that you do not want to be with him, you do not have feelings for him, but you're jealous and upset with the girl he is now dating?" Obviously, she didn't want to respond to that question. The truth was she didn't want to be with the guy; she just didn't want anyone else to be with the guy. Jealousy and competition with this other girl over a guy she didn't even want was bringing out the ugliness in her heart. When jealousy and competition are put before us plainly, they are just nasty.

Side Effects of the Competitive Spirit

The competitive spirit wants you to self-promote and to sabotage others. Bill Johnson confronts us with a scary reality that whatever we gain by self-promotion we must sustain, but whatever God promotes He sustains.[4] If you resort to backhanded ways to achieve your goals, you will actually step out of the place of grace for your life. That is exactly what the Enemy wants. He doesn't want you to see the women around you as community; he wants you to see them as competition. Competitors can be as vile as what we see in times of war. Perhaps they can show some forms of morality, but at the end of the day they are against each other, not for each other. As women we must realize the necessity for women to support other women. We can no longer be content to allow the competition to continue. Ultimately the competitive spirit obliterates unity, which leaves us feeling isolated and alone.

Remember Abby earlier in the chapter? Well, her story wasn't over. After that disastrous living experience with her friends, she received an amazing fashion internship in a different city. The internship put her in housing with three of their models. Abby was terrified of this new living situation. She had obviously never met these women before, but she assumed that since they were models, they were going to be arrogant and competitive. Instead, Abby found that these models were the best roommates she had ever had. They were tremendously encouraging of each other. They never put each other down, they supported each other, and when one of the girls liked a guy, they didn't ever fight over him. Abby was in shock. The most remarkable part is, none of these girls were believers.

One day Abby sat down with Jasmine, one of her new roommates, and had a heart-to-heart about Abby's previous living situation. Jasmine explained to Abby that none of the girls felt the need to compete with her because they weren't insecure in who they were. Insecurity breeds competition. Even though they weren't Christians, these models understood what they brought to the table. They believed in themselves as individuals and in their friends.

If this can be seen among women who don't know Jesus, how much more should it be displayed among us Jesus-loving women? You may not have it all together, but you serve a God who is more than enough for you. You bring a lot to the table, and you don't need to compete with other women for your spot. You have God on your side.

An often overlooked side effect of this competition and isolation is exhaustion. If you're too busy competing with other women, you won't invite them in to help you! We attempt to do for ourselves what was meant to be done in partnership. When we're not afraid of the women around us being "more successful" or "more talented" than us, we'll gladly invite them into our lives and ministries. The competitive spirit hates partnership and wants us all to try to figure it out on our own. No wonder we're tired and discouraged. We're working overtime, burning ourselves out, just because we're afraid that another woman's light might burn a little brighter than ours.

The Cure for Competition

Generosity is difficult when you feel like resources are scarce. That is how I know it's a redemptive answer to the competitive spirit. As believers we get the privilege of defeating the Enemy by partnering with the opposite spirit of whatever he is attempting to use against us. When you feel competitive with another woman, punch the Enemy in the face by being generous toward her.

Several years ago I was in a situation where it was made clear that another woman felt the need to compete with me. Comments were being made both to my face and behind my back that were triggering that old Jessika who'd tackled her brother on the basketball court. That competitive spirit was rising up inside of me, and I kept thinking, "If she wants to go, we'll go!" I know you've never felt that way before, but I humbly admit I still have times when this thought process rises up in me.

As I prayed and sought Holy Spirit about how to squelch both the competitiveness I was feeling and what was being done toward me, He began to speak to me about generosity. The first thing He had me do was recommend her for a speaking invitation that I had been given. Now listen, that doesn't sound like a big deal; however, this was at a time when I was just getting into itinerant ministry. I longed for every opportunity I was given to be in the pulpit, so to decline and give the opportunity to someone who didn't even like me was extremely challenging. It took a lot of prayer and a lot of yielding myself over to finally do as He instructed me—but He wasn't done there. Next, He had me write a check to sow into her personal ministry. I gave her an opportunity that was mine, and He wanted me to financially sow into her. When He asks you to do so, just write the check, ladies. He always has a plan.

Finally, He had me write a list of the characteristics I admired about her and send the list to her. By the time the third task was done, I genuinely felt compassion toward this woman. Honestly, I don't know how He does these things; I am just grateful that He does. He took my competitive, judgmental heart, and through generosity gave me His heart of compassion.

Generosity isn't confined to the realm of money; in fact, many times there are other much more powerful categories to freely give from. As a minister I've found that one of the surefire ways to beat the competitive spirit is to give of my favor and opportunity. When I share doors that have been opened to me, it gives a notice to the Enemy that I will not tolerate competition in my heart, and it also lets other women know that I am unwilling to compete with them: I'm not trying to beat you; I want us both to succeed in doing all God has called us to do. I refuse to glorify what we deem as success over what God calls success. It isn't about how many speaking engagements you have, how big of a ministry you have, how much money you make, what type of house you live in, or any of those other things. Rather, it is about whether you are reflecting Christ in your life. Will you set aside the jealousy and competition to choose to be more like Jesus and love your sisters in Christ with a godly love?

An Alternate Way

I understand the feeling that there isn't enough to go around, and I have experienced innumerable moments when I've felt this way. Over and over, God has brought me back to this one reality: He is my Provider, and other women are not my enemy.

I remember watching *The Hunger Games* for the first time. If you have never seen the movie before, it depicts a days-long battle to the death among men and women in an arena while the world watches. There are twelve territories that each pick two representatives, which they call "tributes," to battle in the games. In the first *Hunger Games* many of the fighters were young and female. As disturbing as the movie is to watch, it brings both sides of the coin to this illustration. You watch people who likely would have been nonviolent in their daily lives become savage in their fight against each other for survival. Countless scenes portray the ugliness of division and competition among mankind. On the opposite side there are beautiful scenes of unity and defending others. At the end of the movie, a young couple, Peeta and Katniss, "conquer" the enemy's plans by refusing to turn on each other. They refused to compete, and so they won.

My plea to you, friend, is to see this ugly attack of the Enemy that has spanned generations, and I'm asking you to refuse to partner with it. Choose instead to partner with gratefulness and generosity. See your sister not as your adversary, but as your teammate. As we go into this next chapter, we are going to discuss the need we all have for community. The truth is, my friend, we are stronger together.

6

More Than Me and Jesus

Call it a clan, call it a network, call it a tribe, call it a family.
Whatever you call it, whoever you are, you need one.

Jane Howard, *Families*

If only I had a nickel for every time someone said to me,
"All I need is me and Jesus!" It is rarely well received when
I respond by explaining that the statement is not biblical. Unfortunately, these types of comments usually come
from someone who has been hurt just enough times to
decide that life would be better if they could live in the
isolation of their prayer closet. I can identify with these
feelings. After one too many betrayals I also have felt that it
must be my life's call to be an intercessor who lives out all
her days in solitude. After all, there is the story of Anna,
who spent decades in the temple praying. "Me and Jesus"
sounds like an appealing future that would undoubtedly
greatly reduce the risk of the stab wounds and backbiting

that are common when we venture out into the world where people reside. The problem with this envisioned utopia is that the Bible doesn't celebrate isolation at all.

"Whoever isolates himself seeks his own desire; he [or she] breaks out against all sound judgment" (Proverbs 18:1). *The Message* offers a less than subtle interpretation of this verse: "Loners who care only for themselves spit on the common good" (Proverbs 18:1 MSG).

Like it or not, the life of a Christian is one that has a heavy emphasis on both our relationship with Jesus and our relationship with others. Jesus explained that the greatest commandment has two parts: to love God completely and to love our neighbor. He asks us to do both, loving vertically and horizontally. Though there is a time to go be alone with just you and God, do not confuse a time of separation to be alone with Him with isolating yourself from community. They are not the same. We can't deny the superiority of our vertical relationship with us and God, but we equally cannot ignore the importance of our horizontal relationships with community. We definitely have a personal relationship with Jesus; however, we were never meant to have a solely private one. This life with Jesus we have been called to live is meant to be lived out with people. The Bible is a book that addresses communities far more often than it deals with individuals. In fact, according to theologian Roger Olson, "The very idea of authentic, vital Christianity apart from the church was virtually unheard of before the twentieth century."[1] The New Testament church would not have understood a concept of private faith. You, my friend, were made for community. For some of you I hear that strong, resounding "Amen!" And for others of you I can literally feel the cringe that just rose up inside. I get it, I really do. I am praying that as you read through this chapter, your heart will release the pain that others have caused you and embrace the biblical call of Christian community.

After I went through a battle with post-traumatic stress disorder, I made an inner vow that I would never trust people again. Through many unfortunate circumstances I had been hurt deeply, and frankly, I had done more than my fair share of wounding others as well. Once I was no longer battling for my life, I decided that we all would be better off if I just did life with me and Jesus. In my new city I had a plethora of surface-level relationships, which included a never-ending list of coffees with people I allowed to have the tiniest little glimpses into my life. I was just never willing to let my walls down enough to be truly seen, or God forbid, ever get hurt again.

One day when I was sitting with my new friend Musy, who happens to still be one of my closest friends today, she looked at me and said, "You need to let people into your life; you need to put down roots. I watch you bounce from friend to friend without ever going deep enough for anyone to actually know you." She gave me a good little lecture for a few more minutes while under the surface I was thinking of the ways I could bail as quickly as possible and never talk to this invasive lady again. As I left her house and journeyed home, I began to feel that ever so gentle, yet firm, nudge of Holy Spirit. In the way that only He can, He spoke to my heart and invited me to open my heart again. As I contemplated my friend's words and poured out my heart before the Lord, I realized that all those walls I had built to keep me safe had also kept me isolated. As much as I wanted to prevent more pain in my life, a topic I discuss more extensively in my book *Trials to Triumph*, I didn't realize that ultimately, by avoiding real connection I was also robbing myself of fulfilling relationships. I have quoted Dr. Brené Brown already, and here again I find myself leaning into her research on vulnerability and wholehearted living to help us find the courage to vulnerably embrace community:

> As children we found ways to protect ourselves from vulnerability, from being hurt, diminished, and disappointed. We put on armor; we used our thoughts, emotions, and behaviors as weapons; and we learned how to make ourselves scarce, even to disappear. Now as adults we realize that to live with courage, purpose, and connection—to be the person whom we long to be—we must again be vulnerable. We must take off the armor, put down the weapons, show up, and let ourselves be seen.[2]

It is not bravery to hide and isolate yourself from others. There is no doubt that it takes some gumption to really put yourself into community. It is, though, quite vital for the call of God on your life that you choose to embrace healthy relationships with other women within community. We actually need you to heal from the hurts you received and choose to play a meaningful part in the body of Christ.

Your purpose from God may have come wrapped inside your body, but it was always intended to be done within community. In Acts 13:36, Luke, the book's author, says of King David, "For David, after he had served the purpose of God in his own generation, fell asleep and was laid with his fathers." Luke shows us that David's purpose wasn't just about David; it was the purpose of God for his generation. It was a communal purpose.

Still today God strategically plans our lives within the context of the people around us. This is difficult for us to understand in our Western individualistic and modern mindsets. God is a God of community. He cares about our relationships with each other. His Word speaks about them constantly. It was so important to Jesus that He even addressed it in one of His final prayers in John 17. He prays to the Father that we would be one, just as Jesus and the Father are one. He takes it even further as He explains that when we, the community of believers, are one—and yes, He meant women too—then the world would know that He was the Son of God. It's as if Jesus knew how divided the body of Christ could become. He also knew that when the bride came together in unity, it would be a sign to the world of who Jesus is. You cannot have community without unity. That unity among believers is a beacon of light to the lost world. Paul addresses this repeatedly in his letters to the New Testament church, urging them to forgive one another, to live at peace, to encourage each other, and to dwell in unity. We are indeed stronger together.

Perhaps this is one of the reasons the Enemy fights so diligently to bring division among us women. He knows there is a purpose that can only be found in the context of community. It's as if he believes more than we do that when we women come together and support each other, nothing is impossible for us. The Enemy would like nothing more than for you to isolate yourself and be left to do life on your own—because you can't. You cannot be all that God intended you to be on your own. Like it or not, sister, you need your tribe.

It has been a privilege to travel around the world preaching the gospel in the nations for over fifteen years. I have spent time preaching in many different settings, from churches with dirt floors and no air-conditioning to sanctuaries with stunning stained-glass windows. It doesn't matter—rich or poor, American or not, there is a longing in the human heart to be known and accepted. Some of you may have been hurt and run away from relationship with other women, but in your heart of hearts you still crave real connection. You were designed for it.

Community Brings Protection

We have all heard it said, "There is safety in numbers!" I was doing a recent study on the behavioral patterns of lionesses. Repeatedly, I kept hearing from other women that it is the time for the lionesses to arise in the body of Christ. (Lisa Bevere has written an entire book addressing the topic, and if you haven't read it yet, grab yourself a copy of her book *Lioness Arising*.) During my own study of lionesses, I found that they hunt together and share the responsibilities of daily life together. It is extremely rare and completely uncharacteristic to find a lioness who lives alone. It is documented that if for some reason a lioness is alone, she displays symptoms of loneliness and is unable to care for her cubs, defend her territory, or catch suitable prey to feed herself. This is astounding because lionesses are the primary hunters in a pack of lions, but alone, she loses the ability to fulfill her role. Being alone makes the lioness a target to her adversaries. It is within her community that she finds protection. It is in that same community that she is able to fulfill the role she was designed for.

It is the same for women. Lionesses hunt together. Lionesses raise their cubs together. Lionesses defend and protect each other from attack. I believe the lionesses have learned what we humans are still trying to figure out. There is great protection when we run as a pack. God meant for us to find a community under the shadow of His wings. I will never opt for a faith that disregards God's role in our daily lives; however, to ignore the role of our community is also ignorant. There is protection as we unite.

We have a common enemy. Satan will attempt to convince you to isolate yourself so that he can corner you alone. That is why Proverbs tells us that we break out against sound judgment when we isolate. On your own you are vulnerable to the attack of the Enemy, but in your tribe you will never fight alone. As women we need to have each other's backs. We need to be women who will go to prayer with and for one another. When the Enemy begins to attack one of our sisters, we should wage war on her behalf.

Unfortunately, many of us have seen the results when we shoot our own wounded instead of picking them up and getting them to safety. Despite what some of our experiences may have been, I believe it is natural inside of women to show compassion and help others in their time of need. We have this superpower of having the compassion of Christ, which goes out of its way to support others who are in pain. You may not be able to get through that difficult situation on your own, but then your sister comes alongside you and fights for you, and you are able to endure. She's got your back.

When you find your tribe of women to run with you, you can rest assured that they won't let you fall down in defeat. They won't let you give up. They won't let you be left behind. One of my favorite things to do is to train women how to run races for the first time. Usually women find the desire to run right after facing a hard season. There's something about coming out of the fire that gives you the desire to believe for more. I like to train with women in that season. Running teaches us a lot about faith and life. Running with other women teaches us a lot about community. No matter how little experience or how much experience you have with running, you are going to have days when you just want to quit. There will be days when even the simplest runs feel impossible. That is why you run with a partner. Thank God when you are having a hard day, your partner is there to encourage you. I have a motto when running: "You can always slow down, but you're not allowed to quit!"

As we run together one day, you may be feeling tough as nails while I am dragging, and on the next day the roles may be reversed. Together we keep going. As we run together, we learn that we are stronger than we ever thought we were, and we can go way farther than we ever thought we could. Together we realize there will be days when I need you to push me because I can't push myself. Sometimes as we train, we learn that some days we need to rest and some days we need to get after it. As we run long distances mile by mile, our minds might tell us that we won't make it, yet we have a friend right there beside us telling us that we will. If I'm the friend, I'm probably quoting some cheesy inspirational quote to make sure you don't forget just how powerful you really are.

Many of us have been told that as a woman all you need is a husband, and then you'll have all the community you'll ever need. Over the years I've realized that this just isn't true. As an unmarried woman, if I was waiting for my husband to be the community I needed, then I would still be waiting. Most singles realize that they need other women, but even my married friends have expressed the desire and need for female friendships. This does not diminish the role of men and husbands; it's just recognizing that women need the support of women too. Women bring support in a different way than men do. We challenge each other and encourage each other in a unique way. We need to recognize our need for female community. We need each other because community protects us and brings out the best in us.

Community Refines Us

Godly community works as a refiner in our lives. As Proverbs 27:17 says, "Iron sharpens iron, and one man sharpens another," or for our sake, "One woman sharpens another." I have always felt that I had the utmost Christlike characteristics like patience, kindness, and humility. They all come just so naturally . . . until I have to be around people. I remember telling a friend one time that patience just wasn't that difficult for me. Only a few short months later my twenty-one-year-old spiritual daughter moved in with me. Out of nowhere I became impatient. I didn't see it coming at all. Before she came, I felt incredibly patient; then she arrived, and everything changed. Usually it was because when I was ready to leave, she still needed to get dressed. Sometimes it was because she insisted on being the one to cook and then wanted help with every single step of the recipe. The scariest moments were when she wanted to drive, and she forgot about a thing called the brake. It's a good tool that all of us should be familiar with. All I know is I was extremely patient when I lived by myself, then all of a sudden she moved in, and I was no longer a patient person. I still blame her for it. You might laugh because you've had a similar experience. You were so like Christ until you were put in a setting where you had to frequently do life with someone else. It's easy to be Christlike alone; it is in community that we are refined to look more like Jesus.

Ladies, we need other women who help us to see the junk that we don't always see in ourselves. Not so they can criticize and gossip about us, but instead so that they can encourage us in our journey of sanctification. Your friends will see your blind spots, and a good friend is willing to gently show them to you. My friend Musy and I made an agreement. You might remember that she is the same one who told me all those years ago that I needed to let people into my life. Our agreement is that any time we see something in the other's character that doesn't line up with the nature of Jesus and the Word of God, then we are allowed to confront each other. We consistently check in with one another to ensure that we are growing in Christlikeness. It is not shameful or guilt ridden; it is full of hope and inspiration. We don't use it to beat each other down or because we want to take part in some twisted game of humiliating each other. I want her to be the best daughter of God, wife, mother, minister, and friend that she can be, and I know that her deepest desire is to be like Him. And vice versa, she knows the same of me. She knows that what I want above all else is to love Jesus with every ounce of my being and to be pure before

Him. This doesn't happen just because we want it to. It happens because we have a friendship and a community that pursues this together with, of course, the help of Holy Spirit. We allow our friends to see us, even the ugly parts, and to call us to a higher standard.

Community Requires Vulnerability

I was recently asked what my personal opinion was on why more women don't have deep intimate friendships that include accountability. The answer immediately came to mind that it's because most of us have so much fear surrounding real connection. We really don't want anyone to see the unholy parts of us. Surface-level friendships feel safer because then we don't have to worry about others seeing our real selves. The "real me" isn't always kind or patient, as my spiritual daughters will tell you. If I really want to be authentic, then it means that you get all the ugly parts too, and ultimately you may reject me for them.

Research tells us that women, more than their male counterparts, strongly desire intimacy in their peer relationships and report high amounts of worry that they'll be abandoned in those friendships.[3] In other words, we ladies strongly desire deep friendship and equally have intense fear surrounding that level of friendship. There is a war of contradiction in our hearts. We already touched on vulnerability in another chapter; however, it's worth repeating that to have true friendship and community, we must be brave enough to be vulnerable and be seen. The refining that comes from community reaches a whole new beautiful level in vulnerability.

We will discuss healthy friendship in a later chapter, so I won't go too deep into it here. Just know that as you choose vulnerability within trusted Christian female friendship, you make space for accountability that brings freedom. On top of accountability, you get to be accepted for who you are. The real you. Not the fake you that you put forward. Not only the parts of you that you think people will like. In vulnerability we get to be who we really are and trust our sisters to love us that way. Listen, we all have certain parts of ourselves that we deem unlikeable. For you maybe it is that impatience that demands a little too firmly that everyone be ready on time (or maybe that's just me). Perhaps it's some weird quirk that you think no one will understand. Lord knows we all have them. I'm not sure what area of your life the Enemy has lied to you about and told you it makes you unworthy of being accepted, but it is just that, a lie.

When we really open up to each other, we learn that none of us is perfect. We all have our areas that we need to grow in. We certainly all have weird things about us. That is the beautiful thing about community. It does require unity, but it never demands uniformity. We do not all have to be completely alike to support each other. In fact, we shouldn't be. We're all different, and that's what makes this so fun. In our journey of community, we're all getting to know each other, both the parts we're proud to put on display and the ones we might be tempted to hide. In that process of learning about each other, we get the highest privilege of loving through it all. I have a friend who loves to eat in the shower. For whatever reason this is a wild trait that even her mother can't understand. The beauty of friendship is that we get to love and accept her, shower eating habit included.

You never know, those things you have been hiding to try to protect yourself from rejection just might be the very areas you need to be seen and accepted in so that you can find healing. God will often hide our healing inside community. We see that demonstrated in James 5:16, which says, "Therefore, confess your sins to one another and pray for one another, that you may be healed." I always found it strange that this verse doesn't say to confess your sins to God and be healed. Instead James points us toward community. There is healing to be found in our vulnerability with community—not just with sin, but in countless areas of our lives. As we open up and let people in, there we find sweet healing.

Sister, I know you have been hurt. I'm asking you to be brave. Let down the walls you've built to protect yourself and let community in again. Trust God to help you find the tribe of women who will be your community. As you open yourself up for deep relationship again, I know that God will bring healing to your heart. In community we become more like Him.

7

Healthy Female Relationships

The best kind of friendships are fierce lady friendships where you aggressively believe in each other, defend each other, and think that the other deserves the world.

Unknown

Women who support other women are confident, generous visionaries.

Mariela Dabbah

It is not enough for us to know that we need to be in community; we need to know how to do community well. Besides hearing about the Golden Rule in kindergarten, I don't recall being given specific instructions on how to actually be a good friend. As I thought about the TV shows I watched growing up, and even more so the ones available today, it's no wonder that when we look around we see a world full of dysfunctional relationships. If you ever caught an episode of *Dawson's Creek* or *One Tree Hill*, you know what I mean. Even though I'm aging myself with those shows, the same goes for most of us—we were not taught how to do community in a healthy way. Our culture makes us assume that lying, competition, jealousy, and manipulation are normal when they most certainly don't have to be, especially for Christians. You can have godly relationships with other women. I will continue to shout this from the rooftops over and over again until we get it. Women can actually support each other.

The Golden Rule is actually always a good start, so thank God for our kindergarten teachers explaining to us that we should do unto others what we wish they would do unto us. It's taken from the Bible in Matthew 7:12, as Jesus is giving His famous Sermon on the Mount, a beautiful guide for how to do life the kingdom way. It sounds quite idyllic, doesn't it? Imagine all of us choosing to just treat others how we wished they would treat us. Relationships that were actually rooted in love, honor, and respect. The type of friends and mentors we've dreamed of being with other women. Relationships in which they know the worst of us and believe the best in us. Kind of sounds like Jesus, doesn't it?

I think sometimes we honestly know what we shouldn't do. Don't lie, don't manipulate, don't be jealous. Surely none of us wants to be treated in those ways. We've discussed some don'ts already in this book, and we have some more to get through, but what about the do's? Just because I know what not to do certainly does not mean I understand what to do. All healthy biblical relationships start with one common denominator, and that is love. If we run every action through the love filter, our relationships would be transformed. Let's take a look at a passage you probably know well, taken from the famous love chapter, 1 Corinthians 13.

> Love is patient and kind; love does not envy or boast; it is not arrogant or rude. It does not insist on its own way; it is not irritable or resentful; it does not rejoice at wrongdoing, but rejoices with the truth. Love bears all things, believes all things, hopes all things, endures all things.
>
> 1 Corinthians 13:4–7

One of the easiest ways to confirm if you are being loving is to stick your name right there in the place of love and see if it pans out. Go ahead and try it out. Can you say, "I am patient. I am kind . . ."? What about "I am not rude, I don't insist on my own way, I am not irritable"? This is about the point where I want to rip that page right out of my Bible. You can even try the action you're contemplating. How about the text that you've typed, deleted, retyped, changed, sent to someone to check, and are still contemplating sending? Is that text patient, kind, etc.? If it doesn't pass the love test, then maybe it should wait until it can.

We can even take it one step further. What about those thoughts you've been running through your head over and over? Are those thoughts of patience and kindness? I'll admit this test is a bit cheesy, but it's effective. The love test is revealing. It has prevented me from doing stupid things hundreds of times. In addition to prevention, it has encouraged me to be the type of person I want to be as well. It's a biblical lens with which I can see whether my heart is in the right place or not.

When I think of the type of woman I want to be, I don't imagine what most consider the stereotypical woman. I dream of a woman who prioritizes other women above herself. A woman of character and integrity who empowers women. I hope I am the type of person who, when anyone talks negatively about me behind my back, those who know me would never believe what is said because of the person and friend I have demonstrated myself to be. I don't think any of us dream of being a bad friend of low moral character who will do anything to get to the top of some proverbial mountain of success. I doubt any of us lay in bed as a young girl dreaming of being a mean girl when we grew up. If you're reading this, I believe that you genuinely want to be a godly woman above all else. So one of the questions I ask myself often is, "What type of woman do I want to be?" Believe it or not, this has a huge impact on the decisions I make in my relationships. Let's look at some of the characteristics that make us a good friend, daughter, mentor, etc. These are characteristics that, when practiced, make for healthy, godly relationships among women.

Trust

One of the most coveted traits in a relationship is trustworthiness. This is one of those areas that women get the most criticism about. In movies and TV shows we see women who gossip, refuse to keep secrets, and are generally known for stabbing each other in the back. We all want to know that our friends are not the type of women who go tell our business all around town. We want friends who are trustworthy. This is a standard you can prioritize for yourself. Make the decision to be a trustworthy friend. Be that friend whom other women can trust to keep private issues private. You can choose to be the friend who refuses to inflate or distort the truth while the world lives in the chaos of internet lies, unscrupulous media, and what has led to the famous catchphrase "fake news." Being a trustworthy person is truly being a light in the darkness. With the uprising of artificial intelligence and the struggle of knowing whether something is real, be someone who is not fake.

I am thankful for the women in my life who are earnestly trustworthy. I can come to them for an honest opinion and know they won't just say what I want to hear; they're going to tell me the truth. I look for women to surround myself with who prioritize truth over just being accepted. When the rubber hits the road, we don't need friends who will say one thing to our face and another behind our back; we need friends who are trustworthy. I don't think we can overemphasize the value of trust in relationships. When trust is broken, the very foundation of relationships is shaken, and we spiral into a world of uncertainty. Where mistrust breeds insecurity, trustworthiness breeds security.

We see this demonstrated in our relationship with Jesus. Years ago in a time of prayer, God spoke to me and said, "Jessika, one of my primary objectives with you is building trust." His statement took me off guard because I thought God didn't need to build trust—He's God! I realized, though, that there is so much God wants to do for me, in me, and through me—but He can't because of my lack of trust. In the Greek, many times the word translated "faith," *pistis*, can also be translated "trust." So God takes the time to build trust with us because He knows great things come when we can trust Him. Likewise, in our relationships with other women, when we choose to be trustworthy, we can get far more out of the relationship than if we continued on in mistrust. We should aim to be trustworthy. A woman of character who says what she means and means what she says. A safe place for our friends and community to trust that they will be loved and respected.

Reliability

Going hand in hand with being trustworthy is being reliable. The Bible tells us that our yes should be yes and our no should be no (Matthew 5:37); however, in today's culture that is rare. I won't have us all count how many times we have said we would do something for another friend and then we backed out. In fact, we all probably have that one friend who says she'll show up, but more than likely she won't. On top of not showing up, we may not hear from her for days. She doesn't mean to do you harm; she just isn't reliable. She isn't trustworthy.

Reliability has become top on my list of characteristics I want in my team and in my friendships. For several years I had female interns to help with my role inside a ministry school at a very large and well-known church. Interns were students in their third year of school. After two years of being mainly in a classroom setting, the third year focused more on practical ministry in their area of choice. My interns and I taught classes, helped my spiritual father and boss in his ministry, and took teams of students all around the world. To put it plainly, we were busy. There were multiple balls in the air at any given time, and my heart was to train these interns so that when they left me, they would be ready to launch into whatever next step of ministry God was calling them to take.

Our school had thousands of students every year that came through, and goodness, they were so hungry for Jesus. It was absolutely beautiful. The thing that always caught me off guard, however, was that as passionate for Jesus as they were, they were known for being incredibly unreliable. It was commonplace to ask for volunteers among students and for only around half of them to actually show up. There was a huge gap between their passion for Jesus and the practical discipline of being trustworthy.

When I chose my interns, this was always one of the first conversations we had. Of course, I understand having emergencies or even days when you might just need a break. We all have those. The issue arises for me when you have an emergency or need a personal day every week, specifically on the day you're needed for your job. When it becomes a pattern, it's no longer an issue of circumstance; the issue is you. You just happen to be an unreliable person. The conversation I had with my interns began with explaining that being an unreliable person means you are not a trustworthy person. The shock on their faces when I had the audacity to assume that reliability and trustworthiness were correlated! If I can't rely on you to show up on time when you say you will, you can just as easily say that I can't trust you.

In our friendships it is the same. If we say we'll pick up a friend's kids at three, then we should be there at three. If we commit to going to a coffee date, we shouldn't wait until one hour before it's scheduled and then cancel. I'll admit I've been guilty of this myself. I hope that when we women make plans, our friends don't have to think, "Well, let's just see if they actually follow through." I think our culture has somehow convinced us that being unreliable is normal, when it shouldn't be. Solid relationships are built by being trustworthy. Do what you say you'll do, show up when you say you'll show up, and if you can't, just be honest about it, but don't be consistently unreliable. If we want to be women who truly support other women, then we have to prioritize being trustworthy.

Kindness

The love test obviously reminds us of this trait, but kindness is also absolutely necessary in healthy relationships. In a secular study about female friendships, women list kindness as the most desirable trait in their relationships with other women.[1] This shocked me. It does, however, speak to how each of us desires relationship with other women that aren't demeaning and critical, but just simply kind.

Kindness is often an undervalued trait. If you've had enough relationships where women have been spiteful and rude, then you understand how powerful kindness can be. It's that friend who brings over medicine and soup when you're sick. It's when your girlfriends fly into town for the funeral of your family member. It's that Venmo that comes through for a cup of coffee after a hard day. Over and again these acts of kindness have a way of turning what was a difficult moment into a memory of friendship. A time when kindness prevailed over pain.

We can see those glimpses of kindness even from strangers. The time that woman was willing to let you go in front of her in the line at the grocery store because your kids were being crazy. It's the one at your new job who stopped to help explain something you didn't understand. The woman who brought an extra baked good to the church lunch just in case someone forgot to bring something, which you did. These moments of kindness remind us of the goodness in relationship. They reveal the heart of the Father working through the women around us.

What a gift to be that example of kindness to another woman. For all of the times when relationships with women have hurt me, I have ten times more stories of when their kindness was on display. These acts of kindness both from friends and from strangers have brought comfort and relief to my weary soul. It's funny how kindness almost feels angelic. What if an entire generation of women decided to prioritize kindness in their dealings with other women?

When I think about some of the strongest relationships I have with other women, they also involve encouragement. There is something I stinking love about women encouraging other women. It just knocks the knees out from under the Enemy's attempts to pit us against each other. Encouraging you means I have to look at you and see the greatness in you. It means putting on my prophetic lens and believing what God says about you. This is one of my absolute favorite things to do in my friendships and with the women I disciple. I love to look them in the eyes and declare over them what God sees in them. Most of us struggle to see what all God has planted inside of us. It's so easy to have our ears constantly filled with the areas we're failing. Women are especially tough on themselves. You can do nine things right, one thing wrong, and you'll replay that one wrong thing on repeat in your head. It's a brutal onslaught of "you should have and could have done and been better." That is why you need encouraging women in your life. They push the emergency stop button on the roller coaster of discouragement.

As women we get the opportunity to take other women by the hand and help them see a different perspective. A dear friend sat me down the other day and asked the question that I think burns in so many of our hearts. She asked, "Jessika, do you think I'm really doing anything with my life?" This friend has been married for over twenty years, has raised a few incredible kids, and has served in various ministry roles spanning decades. She has helped countless people over the years simply by being the type of woman we're describing in this chapter. She has selflessly loved many women, including myself, yet still her heart burns to hear someone acknowledge who she is and encourage her. We get to build each other up. There are enough people and circumstances in this world telling women that they don't measure up. We face plenty of outside narratives that try to convince us that we can't do things. For sure, we all are well aware that we aren't perfect. This is why we need women who encourage us.

My friend Maegan and I have been friends since we were teenagers. With over twenty years of friendship, we have undoubtedly seen the best and the worst of each other. We have walked through the highs and lows of life, seasons of great joy and those of great pain. I was the maid of honor in her wedding, and she has dealt with every guy I've dated thus far—who obviously hasn't made the cut. Her son calls me Aunt Jess, and I believe one day my children will have the privilege of calling her Auntie Maegan as well.

We've had seasons when we've gotten to see each other regularly or even talk every day, and we've had seasons when I've lived in another country and communication was way less frequent. No matter the season, one thing we've always had consistently is that we believe in each other and encourage each other. On those days when one of us doubts if we're a good mother, a good minister, or whether we have what it takes to keep going, there's always a friend to call to remind us who we are and who God has called us to be. Will you be that type of friend for someone else? A friend who is there to encourage and lift up. A woman who reminds others of just how powerful God is in them and through them. One of those women others aren't allowed to quit around because there's just another pep talk coming their way. Be a woman of encouragement.

Loyalty

The final trait we'll look at is loyalty. The definition of *loyalty* is "a strong sense of support or allegiance." I wanted to include this trait because I truly believe our viewpoints of loyalty have been so distorted. We seem to support one of two extremes of loyalty. One says, "You will defend me no matter what, even if I'm wrong." The other says, "I'll be loyal to you as long as the crowd is for you, but the moment you lose the war of public opinion, I'm out."

I think many times in church we've been convinced that loyalty means that I defend you no matter what your choices are. This type of controlling loyalty has led to defending corrupt leadership instead of standing for truth. A blanket loyalty that requires that I support your every action becomes dysfunctional. True loyalty means that you won't throw me under the bus when I mess up, you won't split and run if I fall from grace, but you're also willing to tell me the truth privately when my actions don't line up. When we take the definition of *loyalty* as "a strong sense of support," then it should encapsulate supporting me into becoming the person God has called me to be. It means I won't abandon you in that process. I especially won't throw a stone when you've messed up. I'll support you. We women would do well to be more like Jesus, who drew the line in the sand for the woman caught in adultery as opposed to being the Pharisee who held the stone. Loyalty means that if you get yourself into a pit, I'm willing to help you out of it instead of just handing you a shovel. It takes a truly honorable person who is willing to stand up for grace when the world is yelling to crucify them! Likewise, in this time of social media, when rumors and drama spread like wildfire, the trait of loyalty is highly underrated. At times loyalty is recognizing when a friend is being ridiculed undeservingly. When cancel culture is screaming at us to believe lies and half-truths instead of believing the best, it can be tempting to join the band-wagon without even listening to the side of the one being accused, afraid that we will become guilty by association. Let's be the women who extend a hand of support to those who are being turned on, even if it costs us something. That is real loyalty.

I've seen loyalty be distorted. At times we assume that the best way we can prove our loyalty to one another is by rejecting someone else. Cut to a scene from any teenage girl movie where some of the biggest fights were because a protagonist accepted a girl she was "supposed" to reject. There are those times when we want our girlfriends to hate those who hurt us—I mean, at least the boyfriends, right? It's as though loyalty requires us to choose sides. But the truth is that in the kingdom of God, you don't have to reject one person in order to prove loyalty to another. Kingdom loyalty is being on God's side, not picking sides.

I remember when two of my friends were going through a brutal dispute. They had both said and done some things that weren't Christlike, and their friendship was struggling because of it. Separately both of them came to me, wanting me to essentially pick a side. It is difficult in these instances to be a person who chooses kingdom loyalty. In this circumstance it meant that I refused to choose one over the other. When you choose to be a loyal friend, you aren't agreeing to dislike every person they dislike or avoid friendship with every person they aren't friends with. That isn't real loyalty. It isn't us versus them. Loyalty isn't even necessarily about choosing sides. It is just as the definition suggests—loyalty is about support. When I consider loyalty, I think of women who will support me through thick and thin while continuing to uphold a godly standard. Kingdom loyalty does not expect anyone to violate their conscience in order to prove itself.

We need godly relationships. To have them, we need to start with ourselves. We need to be the women we've needed ourselves in our lives. Women who demonstrate love by being trustworthy, reliable, integrous, and loyal. I'm believing God for a change in the stereotypes about women. I hope for powerful connection between women that reflects Jesus to a world living in relational dysfunction.

8

Ending Codependency

Do we really have the right to take care of ourselves? Do we really have the right to set boundaries? Do we really have the right to be direct and say what we need to say? You bet we do.

Melody Beattie, *The Language of Letting Go:*
Daily Meditations on Codependency

Codependency is a rising epidemic in society today, both inside and outside of the church. My work as a pastor and a leader of the next generation has brought me face-to-face with this issue countless times. The irony of codependency is that what can appear on the outside to be a godly, healthy relationship can, in reality, be destructive. I have seen the consequences of codependency firsthand, where women who were once the best of friends now cannot even be in the same room with each other. My concern is that as the church, instead of offering guidance and preventing code-pendency, we often enable it. It is impossible for us women to support each other in a healthy way if we engage in toxic codependent relationships that ultimately end in division.

It still raises alarm bells in my heart when I hear women say phrases like, "They are my person," "Best friends for life," or my least favorite, "I can't do life without you!" Those sentiments seem so harmless on the surface level, and at first glance, they probably even sound sweet, as if they're declarations of our devotion to friendship. In actuality they are often indicators of codependency, or at the very least, a misunderstanding of how true community and friendship should operate. For a long time the term *codependency* predominately referred to those in relationship with someone who was stuck in an addiction. Over the years it has expanded as we have seen that anyone can have codependent tendencies. It can even appear in various types of relationships from friendships and mentorships to marriages. Due to the many ways codependency presents itself, it is difficult to nail down a precise definition for it. In her book *Codependent No More*, Melody Beattie explains, "There are almost as many definitions of codependency as there are experiences that represent it."[1] One of the better definitions I've seen is by Robert Subby, who describes codependency like this:

An emotional, psychological, and behavioral condition that develops as a result of an individual's prolonged exposure to, and practice of, a set of oppressive rules—rules which prevent the open expression of feeling as well as the direct discussion of personal and interpersonal problems.[2]

The problem begins when we lose sight of the boundary lines that make us individuals. These boundary lines show us what we're responsible for and whom we're responsible to. As we discussed in the previous chapter, you were created to live inside of a healthy community of believers. Codependency attempts to substitute healthy community with an unhealthy soul tie to one individual. Unhealthy soul ties are when two people become so deeply entwined with each other that it causes a dysfunctional relationship. These unhealthy soul ties cause us to prioritize one relationship over the community of relationships. When one person becomes our everything, they take a place in our lives that only God should be in. This is why, at its root, codependency is actually idolatry. We put one person in a spot in our lives that demands most of our attention, energy, and emotions. This one person has influence on the majority of the decisions that we make. I heard a quote one time that said, "An idol is anything you have to check in with before you obey God." This is typical in codependent relationships. Every major decision, and often even minor ones, must be subjected to the other person in the relationship. In some of these relationships it's simply because they do everything together and feel the need to check in with each other. In others, where one person is in crisis or addiction, the other makes decisions based off how the person who is struggling will respond or be affected.

Rarely do these two people start out this relationship thinking that they want someone in their life to be an idol. It happens inconspicuously, one day at a time. At some point it becomes the "norm" of how the relationship operates. I've heard countless women defend unhealthy patterns in their relationship by saying, "You just don't understand; that's how we operate." Codependency definitely makes you feel like it's "us versus the world" and that no one else gets it. No matter how bizarre or unhealthy your relationship tendencies are to others around you, they are your normal, and thus, they seem perfectly healthy to you.

Codependency functions this way because the unhealthy tendencies usually start out in a seed form. In other words, you don't start your friendship on day one demanding that the other person check in throughout the day or inform you of everyone she talks to and every place she goes. You didn't first meet her and say, "Hi, nice to meet you, you're my best friend forever, and now you need to answer the phone every single time I call." If the demands placed in codependent relationships were demanded in the beginning of the relationship, we'd all run! Instead the friendship usually begins with benign intentions and gradually becomes toxic. In the beginning you're just trying to be a good friend, so you make sure you're there every time she needs you. Perhaps you just want to make sure she's safe, so you ask her to text you when she leaves a place and when she arrives. Occasionally you feel jealous when she spends time with other people and doesn't tell you, so you ask that she checks with you before hanging out with another group of friends. It evolves slowly until over time you create your own code of how you operate together. This code is demanding. You wake up one day and realize that you can't go a single day without talking or one person will get upset, you can't make plans without the other person because they'll get offended, and there's an undercurrent of offense where you justify behavior that's ungodly. That's codependency. Eventually one or both people feel absolutely suffocated and overwhelmed. You walk around on eggshells, unsure what might cause the next argument or full-fledged fight. Can you identify with any of these circumstances?

Most of these relationships end in complete division. One contributor to Melody Beattie's book on codependency said, "Codependency is knowing all your relationships will either go on and on the same way (painfully) or end the same way (disastrously). Or both."[3] Often these relationships can't be reconciled as each person involved finds it almost impossible to even be in the same room with the other.

There is so much hurt and offense. I used to look at situations like this and just get mad at the devil for how he weaves his way into what once were godly relationships. After years of meeting with women who have been in codependent relationships, I now realize that although the Enemy is a jerk, sometimes these relationships end because of God. The Lord is so kind and so loving that He refuses to bless relationships that become idolatrous. In His mercy He will remove His grace so that both people must go running back into His arms for healing and wisdom. I absolutely hate watching this unfold; however, I have come to recognize His kindness in it. I don't want us to be ignorant of the dangers of codependency as we pursue healthy female community. For women to support women to the extent I believe we are called to do, we must be aware of how the Enemy uses codependency to sabotage God-ordained relationships.

Codependent Traits

I have discussed codependency in various settings as I teach God's heart for unity and community. When I've broken down the traits of codependency, many women have come to me and expressed that they were in a codependent relationship and didn't even know it. Unfortunately I've spoken to some who didn't realize they were in a codependent relationship until after it had wreaked havoc on their life. Codependency can be like a tornado that rips through every area of your life, destroying anything and everything that it touches. For this reason we're going to look at various indicators of codependent relationships. My prayer is that understanding the characteristics of codependent relationships might help you to recognize these traits in your relationships or those around you. Together we can see the pattern of how the Enemy uses codependency and hopefully prevent ourselves and others from being deceived.

Control

As I said previously, these traits are small and subtle at first, then grow into unhealthy patterns. One of the most consistent traits of codependency is control. This can take on many forms. It can look like one person constantly needing to control the other person, or it can look like both women attempting to control each other. In the early stages we wouldn't call it control, because initially it presents itself as concern or compassion. These are honorable and valuable traits to have. We all want to have concern for our sisters and compassion in their time of need. Don't let this cause you to fear operating in compassion for those around you. It is absolutely necessary that we model the compassion of Jesus; we just need to recognize when our need to help becomes unhealthy.

In many codependent relationships, one person is seen as the one who needs help or guidance, so naturally the other takes on the role of ensuring that she is taken care of. Even when there isn't one victim and one enabler, we can create this scenario where we think that another person "needs" us. To make this distinction clear after our chapter on community, we all need community. We will all have times when we need the help of others, and we should have times when we are capable of helping others. There is a difference between needing a community and needing one single person. The person who needs help does need someone, but it doesn't mean they always need *you*. This has been one of the hardest lessons for me to learn in ministry. Dr. Henry Cloud says it well in his book *Boundaries*: "We are responsible to others and for ourselves."[4]

As a young adult I became a youth pastor in a very troubled and low-income area. Many of the people in our church were in and out of prison, addiction, and other horrible circumstances. The kids who came to our church often had absent or addicted parents. Quickly I became the one who was determined to always be there for them. In and of itself, this is a good and godly thing, but it became dangerous when I began to think I was the only one who could help them. It didn't take long before I slept with my phone by my ear in case they needed me, and I went beyond what I was able to do emotionally and spiritually so that they were taken care of. I helped others at the detriment of my own health. It took a female mentor of mine to sit me down and explain that I was not their savior, Jesus was.

As women we can be tempted to take on the savior complex. We have the bent to be the Good Samaritan, which is a beautiful aspect of the compassion of Christ. This in and of itself is a Christlike characteristic; however, when we take on the role of savior, thinking we can fix someone or that we are the only one who can help someone, we are on a fast track to codependency. To put it straight, that friend might need someone, but that someone does not always have to be us. We are not the savior. Jesus is.

That yearning to be the one who fixes and the one who helps all the time easily slips into control. Our two worlds begin to mesh into one. The most basic form starts with that need to always know where someone is and what they are doing. I call it the "find my iPhone" scenario. There is a neat feature these days where you can add people on your phone and know where they are at any time of day. Although this is a helpful tool for families with children or spouses, in my opinion it is totally unnecessary and often extremely unhealthy in friendships. No one needs to know where you are at all hours of the day. If you are an adult, you do not have to "check in" before deciding to go somewhere with anyone except maybe your spouse. Usually when I say that, a few of my married friends roll their eyes and say not even with your spouse, but I'll let you and your husband decide on that one. When we create an attachment where we are insecure when we are apart, or worse, think we need to control people by telling them what they have to do or what they cannot do, we have crossed a line in our relationship. In adult relationships we are able to make decisions for ourselves, and we have no right to violate that freedom. Again quoting Dr. Henry Cloud,

> Boundaries define us. They define *what is me* and *what is not me*. A boundary shows me where I end and someone

else begins, leading me to a sense of ownership. Knowing what I am to own and take responsibility for gives me freedom.[5]

This freedom is essential in relationships. The feeling that I hear most from women in codependent relationships is, "I feel trapped." When two people become so close that there is no distinction between the two, it feels like a cage you are trapped in. There is such a high level of control that it's as though another person has as much authority in your life as you do. Relationships were never meant to be this way. We have to be aware within our relationships that no matter how close we may feel to one person, we are still individuals. We each have a right to decide how we live our lives. We will be held accountable before God not for how someone else acts but for how we do.

You definitely have a responsibility to help others. It is good to give advice, lend a hand, and be a reliable friend. This does not mean you are responsible for your friends. Only you are responsible for you. Be aware if you are in a relationship where control is used as a way of demonstrating commitment. Loyalty is not demonstrated through control, but through choice. "Choice and commitment are elements of a good friendship."[6]

Isolation

Codependent relationships often become isolated. Two people become so close that they lose connection with those around them. They might hang out in groups from time to time, but they always make sure that they have more than enough time for just them. If there's anyone that one of them doesn't like, then neither can hang out with them. They begin to reject others based off someone else's experience. People begin to recognize that these two are never apart. They will refer to them as a "package deal." If you're going to invite one, then you absolutely have to invite the other because they never do anything separately. Again, this sounds so sweet. These two friends are inseparable and want to do everything together. I think many of us girls have dreamed of having a bestie like this. We wanted to find "our person." Next to the childhood desire for the man of our dreams, there was also the yearning for that best friend for life. The person that you will do everything with. This just isn't realistic for healthy relationships.

If we are to live the life in community that God has designed us for, then we need to be in community, not with just one person all the time. People in codependent relationships will refuse meeting with others or doing activities that God may have called them to do, simply because their partner can't do it with them. Codependency isn't necessarily about closeness; as the name implies, it's about dependence. We are not to be dependent on any one person. The question I ask is "Are you capable of living without the other person?" If the thought of going a week or month without talking to that person causes real anxiety for you, then there might be some codependence.

Admittedly, I was in a codependent relationship one time that I also did not realize was codependent. We did everything together and truly believed that God had ordained our friendship. We grew closer and closer until we honestly just wanted to hang out with each other most of the time. A leader noticed the issue when we began to argue and fight regularly yet still wanted to do everything together. The leader advised me to take three days with no contact. It's laughable when I look back on it, but this sent me into a panic. We were used to chatting throughout the day every day, and I remember wondering what I was going to do for three days without talking to my friend. When I counsel codependent women, I give similar advice, advising them to take days, weeks, usually months apart. This advice is met with massive objection because one or both don't feel like they can spend that much time apart. Inevitably when those relationships blow up anyway, one woman might even begin to have severe depression or suicidal thoughts.

Tim Keller wrote, "A counterfeit god is anything so central and essential to your life that, should you lose it, your life would feel hardly worth living."[7] When a relationship isolates us to the point that we cannot function without the other person, then it is codependent, and that person has taken the spot reserved only for Jesus in our life.

Crossing Boundaries

Those in codependent relationships are so deeply enmeshed in another person's life that they tend to cross natural individual boundaries. There are several common fruits of these codependent tendencies. One or both people become easily irritable. One or both feel like their world is being shaken even though they can't identify why. One or both would say they feel like they've lost themselves. One or both are usually in a season best described as the "dark night of the soul." The relationship that they have invested so much in becomes rocky and unstable. Both parties feel

insecure, like somehow their life and relationship are slip-
ping through their fingers and there's nothing they can
do to stop it. This is the point where I explain that God,
in His mercy, has lifted His hand of grace. By this time
these relationships have crossed many boundaries. Both
people have usually hurt each other and possibly others.
They have mostly ignored certain ungodly behaviors like
jealousy and anger. Some of these relationships have even
crossed physical boundaries.

A friend of mine runs an incredible ministry called Boldly
Beloved that does work within the homosexual community.
She used to date women as well and now spends most of
her time coaching the church on how to walk with people
who are living this lifestyle or trying to leave it. One day over
charcuterie we were discussing some of the ways women
end up in homosexual relationships. She said she would
estimate that about 80 percent of the female homosexual
relationships she'd observed started as regular friendships
built on the longing for companionship that eventually
became codependent. Their lives became so intertwined
that it led to a physical relationship that oftentimes neither
person was initially looking for and sometimes never even
wanted. For some of the women I've walked with as well,
it took crossing a physical boundary before they realized
that their relationship was unhealthy.

What Now?

If you're reading this and you're recognizing that maybe
your relationship or that of someone else you are close
to is codependent, you might be wondering what in the
world you can do to get on track. Codependency is tricky.

It takes various forms and has many layers of dysfunction. My first piece of advice would be to seek counsel from either a professional therapist or a trustworthy leader in your life. I can give some tips for how to proceed, but those who know you can speak specifically to your situation.

My next piece of advice is to have one of those hard conversations we talked about. Look at the behavior within your relationship compared to the biblical values of love and honor. Discuss where and how your relationship got off track and what you need to do to move forward. In some cases it's as simple as reestablishing healthy boundaries where two individuals function within a community. Prioritize Jesus, His Word, and the community above any idea of how your friendship has operated in the past. You can create a new normal if both parties are willing to make some changes. In most cases, though, you need time apart. You have become conditioned to a relationship that is codependent. Likely you have a normal that does not allow for healthy community, but rather always prioritizes the two of you. By taking time apart you can remember how to function without the other person. At minimum I recommend three weeks apart; however, for most relationships I would start with three months.

The objection is usually that there is no way to do this time apart because the two lives are so entwined. If you're able, this is a great time to go on a mission trip, do a ministry school, or make some other commitment that would pull you completely out of that environment for a season. If this isn't possible, pray and seek counsel for a way to separate your lives for a time. After this time of separation, you can reconnect with a mediator. The mediator helps ensure that the conversation stays on track and remains godly. In this meeting you can discuss what the future might hold. I cannot emphasize enough that this should be a decision made with a leader and not on your own. Proverbs 11:14 (NKJV) tells us that "where there is no counsel, the people fall; but in the multitude of counselors there is safety."

We need healthy female community. I know that when women learn how to do relationships in a healthy way, the Enemy is afraid, and you know what? He should be. When women come together in healthy, supportive relationships, we destroy the works of the devil. It is not surprising then that he tries to weave his nasty little devices into our relationships. Over the years codependency has been on the rise. As the church we need to reflect on how we can stop enabling these unhealthy relationships and instead stand for godly relationships. There has also been a rise in the use of the term *covenant relationship*. We use this term to say that we are bonded for life or even to demand a certain level of commitment. Though I am not against this idea, I think we often misuse it. When you are truly in a God-ordained covenant relationship, no one even has to say it.

I have certain friendships in my life that I have had for ten and even twenty years. These are friends I know God placed in my life for a lifetime. In some seasons we've lived near each other and spent lots of time together. In other seasons we've lived in different countries and talked less. The season we were in and the amount of conversation did not change that we were covenant friends. Not one time did we feel the need to write up a contract declaring our loyalty to each other. We just know this is a God-ordained relationship. We are willing and available to be there for and support each other. In some seasons that means coming over in person, and in others it means answering the phone. We understand that we each have lives with one another and apart from one another. We each have other people God has called us to be in relationship with and to minister to. There is no control or unrealistic expectations. There is healthy communication in and out of conflict. Just because we don't spend every moment together, talk every day, or make it to every single life event does not make us any less covenant friends.

My hope is that as the church, we would do a better job of explaining what healthy friendships can and should look like. My prayer is that as we describe godly community, we aren't ignorant of the Enemy's schemes to deceive. If you are in a codependent relationship or have been in one, do not be afraid—there is hope on the other side. You can change and have healthy, godly community with other women. Seek the help you need so you can end toxic codependent relationships and step into God-ordained relationships. Healthy community glorifies God, and you were made for it.

9

Kick Fear Out of the Way

Fear is a self-imposed prison that will keep you from becoming
what God intends for you to be.

Rick Warren

Fear has been discussed at practically every woman's gathering on the planet since Eve cowardly succumbed to the manipulation of the devil. There was a season when I felt like I would vomit if I heard one more message for women that told me I didn't have to be afraid. Now that I am passing on the same message here, I'm certain Jesus is laughing at the irony. Fear is too common and too destructive to ignore as we rally women to step into the fullness of who God has called them to be. Fear places a unique grip on our souls and keeps us from supporting other women or even allowing ourselves to be supported by other women.

It took me way too long to realize that fear impacts each of us in different ways. It might cause one of us to shrink back and be quiet, while it might cause another to be loud and intimidating. In my case, my fear of disappointing God caused me to overwork myself, while in a friend's life, her fear of failure drove her to avoid her purpose altogether. As I've ministered over the years, I've told stories from days spent sharing the gospel to the unreached in war zones and countries devastated by terrorism. After I recount the testimonies of God in these places, without fail a woman will come up to me and exclaim how brave I am. To this day it still makes me chuckle because this girl you think is so brave has been known to belly-crawl while sweating bullets when exposed to open heights. I might be able to go into nations at war, but don't ask me to climb up on your roof. We all have our areas of bravery, and subsequently we also have our areas of fear. Part of this journey of following Jesus is allowing Him to expose our areas of fear and allow His perfect love to conquer it all. *The Passion Translation* puts it eloquently in its interpretation of Psalm 23:4:

> Even when your path takes me through the valley of deepest darkness, fear will never conquer me, for you already have! Your authority is my strength and my peace. The comfort of your love takes away my fear.

I still remember the first time I read that phrase, "Fear will never conquer me, for you already have!" This phrase exemplifies my work in nations at war perfectly. He has won my heart and conquered the fear of death in my life; therefore, fear in this area has no power over me. As we grow in our relationship with Jesus, His perfect love overwhelms us, and that love triumphs over fear.

Fear is deceptive, and it lies to us. Fear's lies have kept far too many of us in cages when we're meant to fly. The nature of fear causes us to shrink back and ultimately sabotage ourselves. This is why the Enemy doesn't necessarily mind what you're afraid of; he just wants you to choose fear over trust. Fear is essentially faith misplaced. Kris Vallotton says, "Fear is actually faith in the wrong kingdom."[1] Fear gives power to the one who does not deserve it and ignores the God who is with us. No wonder the Bible repeatedly addresses the issue of fear.

> Fear not, for I am with you; be not dismayed, for I am your God; I will strengthen you, I will help you, I will uphold you with my righteous right hand.
>
> Isaiah 41:10

> For God gave us a spirit not of fear but of power and love and self-control.
>
> 2 Timothy 1:7

Evidently God is not the author of fear; instead, in His presence fear is obliterated! The author of Hebrews tells us to "fix our eyes on Jesus, the author and perfecter of our faith" (Hebrews 12:2 NIV1984) because as we focus on Him and not on our fear, then we see life from His perspective, the perspective of faith and not of fear.

The Enemy will tempt us with fear in many different ways, and we have to be aware of his tactics. We cannot be content with letting fear direct our lives. When fear is what motivates our decisions, God is not our leader—fear is—and fear is an oppressive ruler.

Fear of Man

The "fear of man" is a phrase that has gained popularity in recent years. It essentially means that we have a tendency to place too much concern on the opinions and actions of other people. For example, we may be afraid to share the gospel because we're afraid to offend a stranger. Perhaps we're afraid to truly be ourselves because we're afraid of rejection. Ultimately "the fear of man" just points to areas where our focus is out of whack. Our attention is more on men and women than on the Lord. Paul said, "For am I now seeking the approval of man, or of God? Or am I trying to please man? If I were still trying to please man, I would not be a servant of Christ" (Galatians 1:10). If I were to guess, I would say every woman reading this book has dealt with the fear of man at some point in their lives. It isn't necessarily about "men," but people in general, and how much we care about what they think or what they can do to us.

The fear of man has run rampant in the era of what has been dubbed "cancel culture." If you happen to say anything the masses disagree with, you run the risk of being cancelled. All too often this can mean more than just losing followers on social media. It can mean hate mail, losing invitations to speak, and a loss of supportive friends. The risk of such extreme rejection has caused many to shrink back in fear and let the Enemy put a muzzle over their mouths. It's the same fear that causes preachers to water down the gospel in hopes they can avoid offending anyone. It is this same fear that causes women to play small when they really need to stand up. We are afraid of the criticisms and judgments that might come. We wonder if people will question our motives. At its root, the fear of man is extremely self-focused. We are so concerned about how we will be viewed or how we will be treated that we almost become a different version of ourselves. In turn, we then don't allow other women to truly support us because we're so focused on not being rejected. The fear of man is so prevalent that Jesus addressed it head on:

> So have no fear of them, for nothing is covered that will not be revealed, or hidden that will not be known. What I tell you in the dark, say in the light, and what you hear whispered, proclaim on the housetops. And do not fear those who kill the body but cannot kill the soul. Rather fear him who can destroy both soul and body in hell. Are not two sparrows sold for a penny? And not one of them will fall to the ground apart from your Father. But even the hairs of your head are all numbered. Fear not, therefore; you are of more value than many sparrows.
>
> Matthew 10:26–31

Jesus was urging His listeners not to succumb to the fear of man, but rather to trust the heart of the Father toward them. To overcome the fear of man, we must take our eyes off people, including ourselves, and place our trust in Him. Jesus encouraged His followers to choose faith over the fear of man even in the face of death! This is part of following Jesus that the Western church struggles to relate to. We are afraid of losing followers on social media while many believers in the world face imprisonment, torture, and death. I have many friends who serve Jesus in conflict zones and closed nations who have been beaten and even lost loved ones due to their faith. Their stories help to put the fear of people into perspective.

Several years ago I was serving in the Democratic Republic of the Congo, a nation that has faced devastating conflict for decades. One day our pastor came home and told us about a tribe on an island that needed to hear the gospel. Many of them were dying because their crops were diseased and no one was willing to help them. After stirring all of our hearts to go and share the gospel, he dropped the bombshell. Oh, by the way, they're cannibals. They eat people. I remember thinking to myself that if he was so concerned, then he could go! I had always told Jesus that I would die for Him; I just wasn't so sure I wanted to be eaten for Him. But I had a choice. I could fear men who could kill the body but could not kill the soul, or I could choose to trust the one who had sent us there in the first place. To fast-forward to the end of the story, our team went to that island—a team of women, by the way—and the entire tribe gave their lives to Jesus. On the other side of the fear of man was the salvation of an entire tribe. As a team we decided that we would not let the fear of what people could do to us stop us from obedience to the Lord. What might be on the other side of your fear of man? Is it possible that your breakthrough is just on the other side of that fear?

Do not let the fear of others keep you from being the woman that God has made you to be. I can assure you that people will not always approve of you. They will not always champion you. They may even criticize you or put you down. I would love to say that everyone around you will be as supportive as I'm asking you to be in this book, but they won't always be. However, you do not have to succumb to fear's tactics. You can choose to trust the one who made you and called you. As you refuse to bow to the fear of others, you can truly let other women support you. You don't have to worry if you'll be viewed as weak or needy. You don't have to be concerned with how other people will react. You can let them in to love you and support you right where you are.

Fear of Failure

The fear of failure does all it can to avoid any type of risk. This fear is a stumbling block because doing anything great in life always involves risk. Some of the most basic desires in life like getting married, starting a new job, and having kids all involve a measure of risk. We are plagued with the questions of whether we can be a good wife, mom, employee, etc. To truly experience life to the full, you must get outside of what feels comfortable and overcome the fear of failure. If you were meant to live inside your comfort zone, then Jesus wouldn't have sent us the Comforter. He knew that life with Him would mean a life of risk, so He provided us with Holy Spirit. As the Bible so clearly encourages us, "Greater is he that is in [us], than he that is in the world" (1 John 4:4 KJV). This is why it involves risk when we share the gospel, pray for the sick, and believe for the impossible. When I look at the lives of the disciples, I can see clearly that following Jesus demands that we overcome the fear of failure.

One thing that annoys me about Jesus (don't worry, He knows I feel this way) is that He is usually far more concerned with the journey than the results. He focuses on the heart over the actions. He's always looking at the parts of the story that I dismiss. I've learned over the years that while I am examining the finished product, He is often asking me how my attitude was in the process. While I am determined to succeed, He is focused on my growth as a daughter of God. When all I want to do is win, He wants me to learn humility. He simply looks at life differently than I do.

This revelation can be liberating if we realize that we don't have to always get the perfect results if we're willing to lean into Him and grow through the process. This was and is difficult for me. Growing up, my dad had a saying that shaped both my brother and me. He would always say, "There is no such thing as trying; you either do or you don't." My dad did not necessarily care how tasks were done as long as they were accomplished. Admittedly I have learned so much from my father that I am forever grateful for, but as an adult, my brother and I have both decided we utterly disagree with this statement. Sorry, Dad. This perspective is especially wrong when it comes to the kingdom. God is less moved by the final results and more concerned with the heart in the attempt. To put it plainly, God looks at success very differently than we do. As we continue in our journey of life, what we might see as failure, God might see as success. God so loves process that many times our choice to step out and take a risk in faith is success to God, no matter what the outcome is.

I was praying about this very topic several years ago when God gave me an analogy for it. When my nephew was born, I would fly from California to Texas as often as I possibly could to be with him. He was my parents' first grandchild and my first nephew, so obviously he was the center of attention at all times. Being the only family member who lived in another state, I did everything I could to ensure that I didn't miss any major moments for my new little best friend. I flew home to try to bribe my nephew into hitting milestones while I was around. As this wobbly, uncoordinated little buddy started to make attempts at walking, I, of course, booked a flight. I would prop him up on his two chubby legs and grab some form of reward to try to coax him toward me.

As babies do, he would take a step or maybe two before his knees buckled under the weight of his disproportionate body. He'd fall straight down on the diaper that was bigger than his head. As he would fall, what do you suppose my reaction was? Do you think that I would run over and begin to scream at him? Chastise his horrible walking abilities? Criticize him because he clearly did not know how to walk? Or perhaps I'd roll my eyes and say that he could not walk, he would not walk, and we should all accept the fate that he would not succeed.

I'm sure as you're reading this, your mother's blood is boiling. It sounds absolutely ridiculous. Only a misguided, ill-mannered, possibly abusive imbecile would treat a child like that. Instead, when he would fall, I would run over to him and scoop him up. I would start praising him. "Look at you, buddy! Look how far you went. You are incredible! What an amazing walker you are." I would call out to my brother, "Jake, your son is brilliant! He is so athletic! He is gifted! Sign him up for sports; he is going to be in the Olympics! He is most definitely more talented than any other baby I have ever seen!" I would gloat and gloat before propping him back up on his two feet to try again. Why? Because I genuinely enjoy the process of his growth. I look at him through the eyes of love. I don't just see where he is at right now, I see where he is going. I know that he is a baby right now, but he is growing. He will continue to grow into a man, and I want him to know that Aunt Jess is there to support him through every part of the process.

If this is how I feel about my nephew, how much more does God feel this way about you? He loves you and He loves the process of your life. I know that God loves process because He sent Jesus as a baby. He could have sent Jesus as a full-grown man, but instead He sent Him as a baby. A baby that pooped, peed, cried, and nursed at Mary's breast. Before He ever started doing miracles or proclaiming the kingdom, He was just a baby, and God loved it! Jesus took the time to grow, and we take time to grow too. You might be afraid of failing, but God is not afraid of your failure. He really loves the process. This is important for us to learn because I cannot always produce the outcomes that I desire, but I can determine to live with a heart that pleases God.

When we kick out the fear of failure, then we can really team up as women and support each other. We can take that leap to go after that big dream and know that we have women around us to champion us on our journeys. I can't help but wonder how many times my fear of failure has kept me from allowing my female support system to encourage me. Sometimes it takes that leap of faith to realize just how supported we really are.

Fear of the Future

When describing the Proverbs 31 woman, the author (likely King Solomon) says, "She is clothed with strength and dignity, and she laughs without fear of the future" (Proverbs 31:25 NLT). It seems like such a unique description. I understand her being clothed with strength and dignity, but why "laughing without fear of the future"? The fear of the future robs us of the ability to experience current joy. The Proverbs 31 woman was able to laugh and enjoy her now because she was confident in the one who held her future. As the familiar quote tells us, "I may not know what tomorrow holds, but I know who holds tomorrow."

Besides a few gifted prophets, we actually cannot predict the future. We don't know what will happen tomorrow, but we know that God loves us and is with us no matter what comes. Jesus promised that He would always be with us so that we did not have to fear our future. As women we can be overthinkers. We want to analyze every angle of what is and every scenario of what might be. We think that somehow thinking through every possibility makes us more prepared, but in actuality it usually just makes us more fearful. Again, Jesus addresses this issue in Matthew 6, when He instructs us, "Do not worry about tomorrow, for tomorrow will worry about itself. Each day has enough trouble of its own" (Matthew 6:34 NIV). It's as if Jesus knew that we would have the tendency to fear the future.

While I was growing up, a friend's mom really should have read Matthew 6 more often. She was one of those moms who worried about absolutely everything possible. The worry could be as big as fearing we might all die in a car crash to even the most minute issues, like whether we had enough snacks for the car ride. It didn't really matter how big or small the issue was, the level of fear was the same. As young adults most of us found it annoying or at least comical. Now, as a grown woman, my heart hurts for her. She lived most of her life bound up by fear of the future. The "what ifs" of life kept her in a prison. That fear of the future kept her from experiencing real joy. My parents taught her kids how to drive because she was too afraid of what might happen as her kids embarked on this new level of maturity. There were many milestones and celebrations that she couldn't enjoy because fears constantly riddled her thoughts.

A letter from Thomas Jefferson to John Adams discussed unfounded fears plainly:

> There are, indeed, [those who are] . . . disgusted with the present, and despairing of the future; always counting that the worst will happen, because it may happen. To these I say, how much pain have cost us the evils which have never happened![2]

As Christian women I know we all aspire to model the Proverbs 31 woman to some degree. I think we would do a lot of good for ourselves, our families, and our community if we would dare to be a woman who laughs without fear of the future. Corrie ten Boom said, "Worrying does not empty tomorrow of its sorrows—it empties today of its strength."[3] We want to be women who can look to the future full of joy with faith and hope, not fear.

Overcoming Fear Together

Fear is best conquered in community. When fear lies to us, we need our sisters to stand beside us. I like to put all the cards on the table with my community and honestly admit whatever fears I have. When we expose our fears, our friends get the opportunity to call out the lies and speak the truth. We also get the opportunity to walk with people through the inevitable hard moments of life. You might be reading this and asking the question, "But what about when fear is legitimate?" Frequently when I teach on fear, at least one person will ask how we handle fear that is based on facts. For instance, maybe your husband does file for divorce, or you took that risk and it didn't end how you thought. Many of us have fear because we have faced real disappointments. It would be ignorant to assume that you have not dealt with circumstances that produced fear in your life. It would be equally careless to tell you that all you needed to do was pull yourself up by your Christian bootstraps and faith your way through it.

When my friend became sick after already beating cancer one time, I could see the fear rising up as she received her second cancer diagnosis. We could not deny that the doctor had found cancer or that the treatment road ahead would be brutal. I am a woman of faith; it runs so deep in me that if you cut me and examined my blood, I think you would find little cells of faith weaved into my very being. Coupled with my faith is an unnerving amount of desire for authenticity. When life comes barreling at us with impossible circumstances, I often find myself in a deep tension of faith and authenticity. How we deal with fear in the midst of real life is much more nuanced than slapping a quote about faith on a bumper sticker and hoping things change. This is why we need each other when fear knocks on our door. Because sometimes that fear is based on a very real and often devastating reality. As believers we have a responsibility both to show compassion to the hurting and also to stand in faith, refusing to let fear overwhelm us. As Bill Johnson says, "Faith doesn't deny a problem's existence. It denies it a place of influence."[4] Even in the midst of difficult problems we can help each other focus on Jesus and His Word instead of the circumstances. Walking with those facing adversity is a privilege and not a burden. It is an opportunity to show the love of Jesus and lend our strength when another woman may not have any. We get to choose compassion and faith over fear simultaneously. As I reflect over the difficult seasons in my life when fear felt overwhelming, I am so grateful for the friends who came alongside me and believed with me. I will never forget how they partnered their faith with mine in those hard moments.

When fear comes knocking at our door, we should gather our community. Together we worship, we pray, we declare the Word of God, and if necessary, we cry those tears knowing that God is near to us when life's circumstances feel like too much. As sisters in the faith, we expose the lies of fear and we lean into truth together. I draw so much encouragement from Philippians 1:27–28:

> Only let your manner of life be worthy of the gospel of Christ, so that whether I come and see you or am absent, I may hear of you that you are standing firm in one spirit, with one mind striving side by side for the faith of the gospel, and not frightened in anything by your opponents. This is a clear sign to them of their destruction, but of your salvation, and that from God.

As we stand together against fear, likeminded in our determination to embrace the truth, we are a sign to the Enemy of his destruction. Together we can conquer fear and the author of it.

10

Woman, You Can Lead!

Rest in your God-breathed worth. Stop holding your breath, hiding your gifts, ducking your head, dulling your roar, distracting your soul, stilling your hands, quieting your voice, and satiating your hunger with the lesser things of this world.

Sarah Bessey, *Jesus Feminist: An Invitation
to Revisit the Bible's View of Women*

As I write this chapter, I want you to envision me on my knees, pleading with you to believe that you can lead. Not even just that you *can*, but that you *should*. We have undoubtedly had a disproportionate number of male leaders to female leaders in almost every sphere of society. We've already discussed the biblical perspective that women are not inferior to men. I understand that men and women are uniquely different. I've been told more times than I can count that men were made better equipped to lead. This comment always causes me to respond with the questions, "Which men?" and "Lead what?"

We've been given many blanket stereotypes that attempt to prove that women are simply ill-equipped as leaders, and supposedly, that is by divine design. According to this logic all men are emotionally steady, and women are illogical and emotionally charged. Funny, that's not what I experienced as I grew up watching Texas football games. Women apparently are always compassionate, or expected to be, and men are heartless. First, I'm not sure why lack of compassion is considered a positive leadership trait, and second, I've met my fair share of women who lacked compassion as well as men who exemplified it. It's even said that men tend to be more goal-oriented than women, making them less likely to procrastinate and more likely to achieve the tasks at hand. If you met my childhood best friend, you would find a woman who has plotted out goals professionally and personally every day of her life since she was young. She is the poster child for goal-oriented.

It's almost comical when we write these generalizations out because we have all met both men and women who don't fit the narrative of these stereotypes. I am not denying that men tend to have some qualities more than women and vice versa; however, it is ignorant and perhaps even negligent to assume there is such a clear delineation between the two when it comes to personality type or even gift mix. There are obvious biological differences; for instance, men cannot have babies, and women, in my opinion, weren't designed to pee standing up. We should not ignore our clear differences, and equally, we should not accept false stereotypes that attempt to limit an entire gender. Unfortunately, the negative criticism I've received about women in leadership roles has come predominantly from women! Ladies, as women we need to support women stepping into leadership roles. When women lead in their God-given spheres, we all benefit.

It's important for me to clearly explain what I'm *not* saying. I am not saying that women are more equipped than men for every leadership role. I'm just saying that men are not more equipped than women for every leadership role. I am not saying that we should pick women over men for specific leadership roles simply because they are women. I am also combatting the thought process that says we should pick men over women for specific leaderships roles simply because they are men. I am not partnering with a prevalent corrupt ideology that tries to convince us that men and women are exactly the same, because frankly, if you believe we're the same, you have to ignore a lot of biology and common sense. We are different, and that is a purposeful decision made by the God of the universe.

Ponder for a second how many types of leadership roles there are all around the world. There are leaders of corporations, sports teams, government positions, organizations, schools—the list goes on and on. If there is a group of any type, then you will most likely find a leader. At times these leadership roles aren't given official titles, like in a family, a friend group, or in a casual game of pickup basketball. As famous leadership specialist John Maxwell says, "A great leader's courage to fulfill his vision comes from passion, not position."[1]

Women who lead from passion and not position are as equally valuable as those who have a position. The realization that we can lead without a title opens up realms of possibilities for where you can step into your God-given authority as a leader. Many women I know believe that only the man should be the leader of the home; however, I watch them lead like a champion with their families. In some cases I am not even sure their homes would function at all without their presence. They might not want to label it leading, but it is exactly what they are doing. I watch as women lead in the church without a title. They step up to meet with members of the congregation who are struggling, provide counsel, and show up for all the birthday, anniversary, and retirement parties. They are leading!

When I was a teenager and received Jesus, one of the parents who volunteered for the youth ministry took me under her wing. She would call me to process what Jesus was doing in my life. She would invite me over for dinner with her family. She spent countless hours leading me closer to Jesus. She never had an official title, and still she was a leader! This is not a plea for every woman reading this to take an official position, though that is important too. It is an urging for us to begin to lead right where we are. The reality is we need female leaders both in positions with titles and in those without them.

We need women to recognize that they have gifts and qualities that need to be brought to the leadership table. You specifically have aspects of who you are that other women and even the world needs. If you believe the lie that you are not gifted to lead, then you will hide these talents and assume that someone else will do what you've been equipped to do.

Leadership is a broad term. *Webster's* defines *leadership* as "the office or position of a leader," "capacity to lead," and "the act or an instance of leading."[2] Under this definition I could possibly be considered a leader when I choose to ignore the street sign that tells me not to walk and instead barge across the road followed by a group of hesitant walkers who were waiting for someone to give them permission to break the rules. This definition might be more accurately applied to when I was in an airport overseas after a redirected flight leading a pack of foreigners who were confused about where to go to be rebooked. In either circumstance there was no election or even a review of qualifications. True leaders seem to lead wherever they go without anyone giving them a name tag or title. This might be why the 1828 Webster's definition included in their definition of a leader, "one who goes first."[3] John Maxwell says that a leader "knows the way, goes the way, and shows the way."[4] Within all of these definitions of *leadership* there is no requirement of a gender or a title. As women we have a role as leaders, and the world is hurting from our lack of intentional female leadership.

Numerous studies over decades of research have proven that women leaders can actually increase productivity, foster an environment of fairness, promote organizational dedication, and even improve group collaboration. Despite all the research that shows women as strong leaders, people still question women's effectiveness in leadership.[5] According to one study, female leaders are more likely to epitomize the positive attributes of an organization and inspire others to do the same.[6] This research is fascinating as it reveals that despite what we have been told, women demonstrate and effectively influence others around them to be exemplary contributors to their environment and community. I have seen this in my own life as a leader. When I am in a leadership setting, my heart longs to be a role model. I begin to ask myself more regularly if my decisions are above reproach and if I am modeling what I want to see in the people I lead. When we have leaders who don't just tell us how to behave but show us how to behave, we become more inspired to meet the standard. As women of God we can take our leadership lessons from the greatest leader ever, Jesus. He taught His followers many keys about leadership, leading by example and contrasting godly leadership with that demonstrated by the religious leaders of the day. When we step into leadership roles, we need to lead fairly with honor toward others.

> Then Jesus said to the crowds and to his disciples, "The scribes and the Pharisees sit on Moses' seat, so do and observe whatever they tell you, but not the works they do. For they preach, but do not practice. They tie up heavy burdens, hard to bear, and lay them on people's shoulders, but they themselves are not willing to move them with their finger. They do all their deeds to be seen by others. For they make their phylacteries broad and their fringes long, and they love the place of honor at feasts and the best seats in the synagogues and greetings in the market-places and being called rabbi by others."
>
> Matthew 23:1–7

Jesus points out that some leaders say, but do not do. They require much from those they lead that they are unwilling to do themselves. Many of us have had negative experiences with leadership in and outside of the church. We've seen those who love the position of leader more than they love the people they lead. We've witnessed those who treat others like tools to accomplish their own goals. When people are viewed like objects, it is not surprising that dishonor can run rampant. We tolerate belittling others, unrealistic expectations of productivity, and a complete lack of compassion. This is why so many people use the word *hypocrite* when describing Christians or Christian leaders. They struggle with the disparity between what we tell others to do and what we actually do.

Leading by Example

One of the deepest passions of my heart is to see a generation of women who lead not just in their words, but in their example. I believe we can be leaders who lead by example. I would love to see us even raise the bar for leaders. This isn't a perfectionist mentality. It often presents itself as quite the opposite, actually. In our attempt to lead by example, undoubtedly, we will make mistakes. But you do not have to be perfect to be a great leader. Making mistakes gives us a wonderful window of opportunity to demonstrate the kingdom value of repentance. As leaders, when we mess up, we can humbly confess our error and ask for forgiveness. This is a beautiful representation of godly leadership, one that unfortunately isn't always demonstrated.

In this season of life, I felt God deeply impress on my heart to do what I call life-on-life discipleship. What that means is that some girls I disciple actually live with me. Let me assure you that when you live together, you cannot cover all of your flaws. What you can do is be quick to repent when your character doesn't line up with Christ's. When we are willing to repent, we build trust with those who follow us. It destroys the pedestal that we sometimes put leaders on and instead shows us leaders who are human and willing to own their shortcomings. People can trust a leader who is authentic and honest with them.

There was a day I just felt absolutely irritable. I know this is shocking, but don't worry, it has only occurred this one time, as I'm sure you can remember that one time you were grumpy. On this particular day it just happened to be that time of the month, multiple things were going wrong, and I snapped at one of my spiritual daughters. I was rude and abrasive. Everything in me wanted to justify my behavior and continue on with my miserable day. Holy Spirit had other plans. He told me to go and repent to her. I wish I could say that was easy. My flesh was screaming all the reasons why I did not need to repent. It was her fault that I snapped, I was the leader and I shouldn't have to be the one who apologizes, and don't forget about those stupid hormonal mood swings. Only for obedience's sake I went and apologized. I explained that I'd had no right to treat her the way I did, and I asked her to forgive me. Immediately her eyes filled with tears, and I contemplated whether my earlier words had been even harsher than I imagined, but that wasn't the case. When I asked her why she was crying, she explained that no leader had ever apologized to her before. Well, just melt my irritable heart. I understood then that few leaders realize the power of repentance. This is the type of women leaders we need right now.

In comparative studies, women leaders were more likely than men to treat people fairly. In fact, in one study the mere presence of a woman in leadership led to people expecting fairer treatment.[7] This flips the script on some stereotypes we have been told, like assuming that women are judgmental or hold grudges. You can trust women leaders to be fair. As women leaders we lead with compassion and fairness. This means that we do not demand respect; we earn it by how we treat those around us. We can make a positive impact on our environment by stepping up to lead and treating people as children of God, just like Jesus modeled.

Dealing with Pride

Another negative attribute Jesus addressed in the Pharisees was their thirst for recognition and how they used their leadership to feed their own pride. In a culture that is extremely ego driven, we need leaders who walk in humility. Pride attempts to put its icky, demonic fingers into every gathering of believers, so it is not shocking when it goes for the leaders. There was a season of my life when everything I was doing was flourishing. Ministry opportunities were abundant, and—just being real with you—I truly felt like I was crushing it at life. One day Jesus gave me the opportunity to be truly humbled. He said to me, "Jessika, pride is an infection that infects everything in you if you leave it untreated. You must war against your pride." This was one of those moments when His words truly brought the fear of the Lord on me. I felt the urgency to not apathetically pray that I would be humble, but rather to resolutely pursue humility with the determination of a gazelle fleeing a hungry lion. Pride destroys us, and it is too widespread among leaders.

Pride convinces you to serve so that you can be applauded, when Scripture clearly tells us to hide our good works (Matthew 6:1). For this reason, as leaders we need to be cautious of how we share testimonies or even post on social media. We should monitor our heart motivations to see if our reason for sharing is to bring glory to ourselves or to bring glory to Jesus. We even need to beware of that comparison bug that comes with social media, where we attempt to find where we are in the pecking order, looking at what other people are or are not doing to see if we appear better than them. All of that is pride as well.

As we lead we need accountability that checks if we are attempting to build our own platform or to truly exalt Jesus. At times the two look so similar that only you and Jesus can know the true condition of your heart. David knew the temptation to hide sin in his heart, where no one else except God could see, so he prayed, "Search me, God, and know my heart; test me and know my anxious thoughts. See if there is any offensive way in me, and lead me in the way everlasting" (Psalm 139:23–24 NIV). David asked God to expose the places of pride in his heart that would keep him from leading in humility because pride would like to convince you that you are always in the right. We become vulnerable to deception when no one around us is allowed to counsel us or hold us accountable because we think we as the leader know better. Pride exalts you above those you lead. Jesus, the only one who has ever had a right to have even an ounce of pride, still chose humility.

> Do nothing from selfish ambition or conceit, but in humility count others more significant than yourselves. Let each of you look not only to his own interests, but also to the interests of others. Have this mind among yourselves, which is yours in Christ Jesus, who, though he was in the form of God, did not count equality with God a thing to

be grasped, but emptied himself, by taking the form of a servant, being born in the likeness of men. And being found in human form, he humbled himself by becoming obedient to the point of death, even death on a cross.

Philippians 2:3–8

This is Jesus, our perfect leader who demonstrated how to lead from a place of humility. People at times assume that humility is weakness, but all you have to do is look at Jesus to know that humility is not weakness; instead, it is a great display of true strength.

Humility understands that even if you are the leader, everything you do well is by His precious grace. At its core, humility recognizes our ultimate dependency on God. It is difficult to faithfully lean into dependence on God and have a prideful estimation of yourself. His holiness, greatness, and perfection bring humility to us. This is why Jesus was so radically humble. Even though He was the Son of God, He was still dependent on the Father. He even said in John 5:19 that "the Son can do nothing of his own accord, but only what he sees the Father doing. For whatever the Father does, that the Son does likewise." Pride tells you that you are able to lead and live on your own. Humility tells you that you need God! Godly leaders will faithfully commune with God.

One of the best ways women can support women is by modeling how to prioritize Jesus above everything else in our lives. We put Him before ministry and even relationships. In the prayer closet, we learn how to fight for other women. We hear from heaven when to be loud and when to be silent, when to sow and when to reap, when to push and when to rush. Women leaders who are built up in the secret place with Jesus are unstoppable forces. That is why humbly making communion with God our highest priority is such a big deal.

This is one way we acknowledge to God how much we need Him, and it is how we model for other women what it looks like to live a life that makes Jesus number one in all things.

This is where leaders can get so far off track. If we get so busy that we neglect communion with God, then pride will begin to grow. We sacrifice the prayer closet for tasks and wonder how our heart grows cold toward God and toward people. Martin Luther said, "I have so much to do that I shall spend the first three hours in prayer."[8] Luther took seriously what Jesus said in John 15:5, that apart from Him we can do nothing. Pride would love for you to think that you can carry your responsibilities on your own, because then you will exchange time with your source, Jesus, for time to accomplish your agenda.

Around the time of that season when Jesus told me that pride was like an infection, I was utterly exhausted. It was the type of tired that doesn't get fixed from one night of sleep. I was busy doing so much kingdom work, from traveling and preaching to missions and discipleship. Every day I was doing what I assumed God wanted from me. The more productive I became on the outside, the less time I was spending alone with Jesus. As a result, I was tired and often felt overwhelmed, unsure of how I could keep up with all the demands. I remember reading the beginning of a familiar passage, "Come to me, all who labor and are heavy laden, and I will give you rest" (Matthew 11:28). It's a beautiful promise for us when we are weary. I read it and wondered how I had believed that doing all of these ministry activities was the same thing as coming to Him, yet I was still feeling exhausted. It felt as though I was experiencing the opposite of what the verse promised. Then Holy Spirit urged me to finish reading the passage.

> Take my yoke upon you, and learn from me, for I am gentle and lowly in heart, and you will find rest for your souls. For my yoke is easy, and my burden is light.
>
> Matthew 11:29–30

The rest comes when we take on His yoke. He tells us to learn from His model of being gentle and lowly in heart. Some translations actually say, "for I am meek." Jesus is saying that His yoke is humility, and that yoke is easy. Have you ever thought about why? Why is the yoke of meekness so easy and light when life often feels quite the opposite? Well, if meekness and humility mean that we are dependent on Him, then we learn that we cannot carry the load ourselves. We prioritize dependence. We make time with Jesus one of the nonnegotiables in our lives. Time with Him to lean into who He is and who He says we are. Moments when we cast all of the load of life onto Him and effectively tell Him that we cannot do this life alone. We need Him. We are totally dependent upon Him. That level of humility is light because there He carries the burden. In that place we have a clear estimation of who we are, and our pride is destroyed. Pride is a heavy burden to carry, but humility is light.

When we women lead from a place of humility, then we destroy pride's poison. Unfortunately, we are all too familiar with pride in leadership. We need the humility of Christ demonstrated by those who lead. Women who will depend completely on God and not on themselves. Those who will not lead for selfish ambition and the applause of man. Imagine with me the power of a generation of humble leaders who will lead for the glory of God and not for themselves. This type of humble leadership will be transformative in our environments and in our culture.

When women step into their place of leadership, we will stop seeing the damage done when we simply place a man in leadership because of his gender. Women are called to lead, and we need what women carry in many spheres of leadership. As a woman I implore you to stop criticizing and tearing down women who believe they are called to lead, whether in a position with a title or not. Let us champion our sisters who are brave enough to lead. We can encourage them to lead with humility and by example. You are not unqualified because you are a woman. You do not need to abdicate God's calling on your life to someone else. Step up and lead, sister; step up and lead.

11

Apostello: A Vision for the Future

> Behind every successful woman is a tribe of other successful
> women who have her back.
>
> Unknown

Without a vision for the future, we will continue in the
same patterns we've always followed. Several years ago
the Lord began to speak to me about the next season in
the church. He gave me a word about a multigenerational
revival in which both male and female, young and old,
partnered together to see God move in our communities. I wholeheartedly believe we all have a part to play in
what God wants to do corporately throughout the body
of Christ. What we often dismiss as we pursue communal
moves of God is the need for individual participation.
For instance, I know many people who pray earnestly for
revival but don't disciple anyone. If we want to see authentic revival, then we simultaneously need intentional

discipleship. As we look forward to where God is taking us, it will require women to step up to the plate and invest in the next generation of women. It isn't enough to just support our female peers; we must become the mothers and big sisters for the young women around us. When I dream about the future for women in the church, I see a beautiful picture of healthy, empowered, thriving women who treat each other like family.

In 2023 I returned to the States after living several years in Brazil. Moments of transition can be challenging, and this one was no different. I left a job and mission that I loved to follow the leading of God back to the States, where I essentially had no idea what God had in store. The projects for the ministry I had were all in Brazil, so upon returning I wasn't sure the direction to take in ministry or even where I would live. Even now, I still get a bit of a nauseated feeling in my stomach when I reflect on this time. As I was praying and trying to make some decisions, my spiritual mom offered for me to live with her until I heard from Jesus about what was next. She definitely exemplified what it looked like for women to support women in this season of my life. She didn't just tell me she believed in me; she showed me by literally bringing me into her house and, of course, feeding me. Food is the universal language of love. We would do ministry together and have daily chats about life and Jesus over coffee. What was meant to be just a three-month transitional time turned into nine months. It was transformational for me.

Over these months God deepened my conviction that we desperately need women to truly support women and to pour into the next generation. One day as I prayed,

God told me that He wanted an army of women who would walk in both the power of God and the character of God. In many Christian circles we tend to emphasize one and ignore the other. It's the equivalent of lifting weights with one arm and allowing the other to atrophy. Within some circles we glorify the use of gifts while diminishing the value of developing Christlike character. There's a problem when we have women who pray for the sick and evangelize yet gossip like it's their second language. It is frightening that we have taught a generation how to prophesy but neglected teaching them how to steward their finances with generosity and integrity. In other circles we do an amazing job of prioritizing spiritual disciplines like Scripture memorization but often overlook the importance of encounters with the power of God. We need women who will disciple women to grow in both the power and the integrity of Christ.

The stereotype that women are jealous and competitive grieves my heart because it prevents many young women from believing there are any women who are willing to invest into them without ulterior motives. I took a poll of some of my female friends in ministry and asked them if they had ever been discipled by an older woman. The responses were mixed, and honestly, I was shocked by the feedback. Overall very few had ever been mentored by another woman. Of the ones who had, an even smaller percentage had an older woman consistently invest in their lives to help them grow as a Christ follower or in whatever the specific call of God for her life was. Several of the women expressed that even though some women had committed to pouring into their lives, there were still times when it felt disingenuous.

Unfortunately we haven't created a healthy culture around discipleship or spiritual parenting. This results in women being somewhat apprehensive about inviting another woman into their lives to disciple them. Many people use the term *spiritual parenting* to describe a close relationship between an older believer and a younger believer they disciple. The terminology is used because of the many occurrences of familial language throughout the Bible, one of the primary instances being when Paul addresses the Corinthian church: "For though you have countless guides in Christ, you do not have many fathers. For I became your father in Christ Jesus through the gospel" (1 Corinthians 4:15). The apostle Paul realized there wasn't a lack of leaders; there was a lack of fathers. I would say it's similar today—it isn't about lacking women who lead, it is about a void of women who will be true mothers in the faith.

For the Mothers

If we want to see a change in how women support women, then we need to start raising up women who have been taught how to truly support other women. We need a massive movement of women who will lead the charge to spiritually mother a generation. You don't have to have it all figured out. You don't need to have the answer to every question. You don't need to lead a ministry. You don't even have to be a biological mom. You just need to be willing to support younger women with the heart of a mother. Here are a few characteristics of healthy mothers:

- A mother loves unconditionally.
- A mother guides.

- A mother corrects.
- A mother encourages.
- A mother empowers.

Here are some things healthy mothers do not do:

- A mother does not compete with her daughter.
- A mother does not sabotage her daughter.
- A mother does not stifle her daughter.
- A mother does not beat down her daughter.

Healthy moms focus on nurturing their children and helping them grow into who God has called them to be. It is key that we don't try to make them into our followers, but rather point them to Jesus so they grow as His disciples. Mothers want to see their children succeed; they are their biggest cheerleaders. I grew up playing sports, and my mom was one of those moms who never missed a game. This woman was a literal cheerleader in high school, so although she understood hardly a lick about basketball, she was the loudest in the gym. If I made a good play, there was no question as to who my mom was. She made it very clear to everyone that I was hers and she was proud of me. Imagine if spiritual moms treated their spiritual daughters this way. For too long we've used the term *spiritual mother* for women who did not choose to love their "daughters" like Christ. Instead of being supportive, they chose competition. We are going to change this narrative.

As a woman who is confident in your God-given identity, you can take a younger woman under your wing and love her as you would your own child. I would not be who I am today if it wasn't for the women who were willing to do this for me. Several women throughout my journey recognized the call of God on my life and chose to partner with Him to help me grow. When I consider their belief in me, I think of what Paul said to Timothy: "This charge I entrust to you, Timothy, my child, in accordance with the prophecies previously made about you, that by them you may wage the good warfare" (1 Timothy 1:18). Paul knew the prophecies spoken over Timothy and viewed him accordingly. He took the time to remind Timothy of those prophecies and, like a father, empowered him in that journey. Not one time did Paul seem concerned that Timothy might outgrow him or overshadow him. He loved seeing Timothy succeed. We need mothers who will celebrate the success of their daughters. I'll never forget when a spiritual mother said she wanted her ceiling to be my floor. I was in shock to see another woman in ministry who truly wanted me to go further than she had. This is the privilege we get as mothers—to see our daughters fly higher and farther than we can.

For the Daughters

Building spiritual family takes more than just having women who are willing to mother. It also means we need young women who are content to be a daughter. Paul said something beautiful of Timothy in Philippians 2:20–22 (NIV):

> I have no one else like him, who will show genuine concern for your welfare. For everyone looks out for their own interests, not those of Jesus Christ. But you know that Timothy has proved himself, because as a son with his father he has served with me in the work of the gospel.

Not only did Paul recognize the prophecies over Timothy's life, but he also saw that he was willing to serve the cause of Christ and thus Paul's ministry without selfishly seeking his own interests. Timothy submitted to Paul as a son. As mothers rise to the challenge of selflessly guiding a younger woman, a younger woman must also be willing to position herself as a daughter. We as women, young and old, must also be willing to serve the older generation as daughters.

This can be a challenging concept for a culture that is so individualistically minded and self-focused. In many ways the younger generation hasn't been taught what it really means to be part of a family. When we choose to submit to being a daughter, it means we need to learn to trust our spiritual mom more than we trust ourselves. We must trust that they have our best interest at heart. Knowing that they love us and care for us gives us the ability to trust them when they correct us or even say no to things that we might see as a great opportunity. I've seen many young women today who want the benefits of being a daughter without positioning their heart as one. They want the promotion, they want the inheritance, but they don't want to be told what to do. Sometimes they are willing to ask for advice but will only apply it if it lines up with their desires. This isn't how we should treat mothers in the faith.

Daughters Serve

Years ago there was a woman I really admired. I desperately wanted more time to be around her and learn from her. I was a lot shyer then than I am now, and I was afraid to just ask her to invest in me. I began to pray daily for

God to show me how I could have this woman mentor me. One day as I was praying, I heard the Lord say two simple words, "Serve her." I remember thinking that I didn't want to serve her; I wanted her to invest in me! I knew for sure what Holy Spirit had said, so I went to her and offered to wash her car every week. I had noticed that she liked things to be clean and organized, so I figured, who wouldn't want their car cleaned for them? Every Thursday I would wash her car, vacuum it, and then return it to her driveway. After doing this for a while, she invited me to stay for dinner on Thursday nights after I cleaned the car. Through those dinners she learned about my heart for ministry and began to give me opportunities to serve in the church. Through that process this woman became a spiritual mom to me. As a daughter I continued to serve her both in the home and in the church.

As our relationship continued, she taught me many things from how to cook certain recipes to how to pray through life's challenges. To this day I put into practice many things I learned from her over a decade ago. This didn't happen because I demanded she invest into me without it costing me anything. This started with my choosing to serve her in whatever capacity she needed. Many times as daughters we approach older women with completely selfish motives and wonder why those relationships don't work out. We must be willing to humble ourselves and serve.

Daughters Listen

Beyond serving, we must also be willing to listen. Many young women are afraid to have a spiritual mom because they think that means they will have a dictator in their lives who restricts them, but let me tell you from personal experience, it is challenging to mother a young woman who thinks she is always right. If you are always right, then why do you need a mother to help guide you? We all have our blind spots, and these spiritual parenting relationships help guard us from the harmful consequences of those blind spots. A good parent addresses those areas where we are weak or even flat-out wrong. They speak to our circumstances in life and guide us in the godly way. A healthy adult parent is not going to attempt to control your every move. Submission doesn't mean that we become a dog on a leash who follows every command without question. It means we trust our mothers and listen when they have guidance for us. We get to have conversations and hear their godly input. Ultimately their guidance protects us and assists us in our journey to fulfilling our God-given purpose.

Multigenerational Relationships

I don't think we ever grow out of the need for a mother. As we get older, we should undoubtedly step into the role of mothering, but it shouldn't stop us from being a daughter. One of the greatest gifts in this season of life has been the moments when my spiritual mother, my spiritual daughter, and I all get to be together. Sometimes that looks like ministering together somewhere around the world, and many times it just looks like eating dinner together. One of my spiritual daughters has affectionately started calling my spiritual mom her grandma. Admittedly that wasn't well accepted at first for obvious reasons; however, now it has become a title of affection. In a biological family we all gather around the table as a unit. We understand that there are different roles, and each family member has their own part to play. I've never met a healthy family where mothers and daughters felt the need to compare themselves or judge each other. You don't see them jockeying for a position in the family. When we come to the table as a family, we're there to support and love each other unconditionally. This is how healthy natural families function, and it is how healthy spiritual families should function.

We are discipling daughters who will then disciple daughters. Together we create kingdom family. The psalmist understood this concept: "So even to old age and gray hairs, O God, do not forsake me, until I proclaim your might to another generation, your power to all those to come" (Psalm 71:18). A research study found that only 27 percent of young people who were prodigals had close personal friends who were adults from their faith community while growing up, but in stark contrast, 77 percent of resilient disciples had these relationships.[1] This study illustrates the power of intentional discipleship to grow committed, active believers who are in it for the long haul.

That is our ultimate goal. Not just to produce churchgoers, but to see committed disciples of Jesus who serve in the family. In the family we are able to raise up mature disciples who can weather the storms of life and stand strong in the midst of opposition and persecution. In their book *Faith for Exiles*, David Kinnaman and Mark Matlock give keys for discipling the next generation. One of the main practices they suggest is to forge meaningful intergenerational relationships, going against the grain of the norms of isolation and mistrust between generations.[2]

To break out of the stereotypes among women and truly see a change in how women support each other, we need to see relationships built between mother, daughter, aunt, sister, and grandmother alike. If we want to see the kingdom advance, we must prioritize multigenerational relationships.

Apostello

We named our new ministry Apostello. *Apostello* is a Greek word that means "to send out." It is used in the context of sending one out in authority or with covering. Apostello was the word used when Jesus sent His disciples out to bring the kingdom of heaven to earth. As we seek to be women who support each other, we have the privilege of building a kingdom family that raises up disciples and sends them out to be representatives of the kingdom of heaven! Paul describes it well in Romans 10:14–15, where he also uses the word apostello:

> How then will they call on him in whom they have not believed? And how are they to believe in him of whom they have never heard? And how are they to hear without someone preaching? And how are they to preach unless they are sent? As it is written, "How beautiful are the feet of those who preach the good news!"

This is our charge. To support each other as family. To be mothers and daughters. As we learn to be a family, we empower one another to step fully into the calling of God on our lives. We aren't sending you out alone; you're going with a family behind you. A family who believes in you and wants you to succeed. A healthy family who will navigate the challenges of life with you. This is how we really support each other as women when we learn how to treat one another as family.

As we apostello, we prioritize this kingdom truth: Jesus described two great commandments. The first is to love God with all your heart, all your soul, and all your mind. The second is to love your neighbor as yourself (Matthew 22:37–39). If these are the two greatest commandments, then as His children we should make following them the two greatest priorities of our lives. As we prioritize loving God with all that we are, the natural response is to love our kingdom family, our kingdom sisters, as we love ourselves. I truly believe that we are getting a revelation of the depth of love that Jesus asks us to have both for Him and for each other.

As we move forward, creating a kingdom family that reflects the heart of Christ, we will see a generation of women who are unfamiliar with the stereotypes that women used to have. I pray that when I have my own biological daughters and granddaughters, they will be categorically unfamiliar with the stereotypes that used to typify women. Instead they will describe women as kind, empowering, forgiving, and supportive. As they grow up in the church, I believe they will develop healthy relationships with other women where they feel known and loved.

When women support each other and develop these strong kingdom bonds, we can and will boldly step into the fullness of God's calling on our lives. We can trust that we are sent out in authority and covering. This is why we apostello. Because we believe there is a new future for women. A future with supportive female relationships that empower us to be all that God has called us to be.

Acknowledgments

✦ ✦ ✦

There are several people who made this book come to life. I am super grateful to my powerhouse team of women who let me verbally process every detail and continually provided support: Giulia Mynssen, Musy Hart, and Maegan Hensley. Thank you for your support.

To the Chosen team, especially David Sluka, there is no way this project would have come together without your advice and continual belief in me.

Also, to the many women who shared your stories with me in the process of writing this book. I'm thankful for your honesty and vulnerability.

Notes

Chapter 1 The Greatness of a Woman

1. "About Elisabeth," archived September 26, 2018, at the Wayback Machine, https://web.archive.org/web/20180926172332/http://www.elisabethelliot.org/about.html#expand.

2. "Quotes," Ameliaearhart.com, accessed August 17, 2024, https://www.ameliaearhart.com/quotes.

3. Jerrie Mock, *Three-Eight Charlie: 1st Woman to Fly Solo Around the World*, 2nd ed. (Phoenix: Phoenix Graphix, 2013), 32.

4. Tilar J. Mazzeo, *Irena's Children: A True Story of Courage* (New York: Gallery Books, 2016), 262.

Chapter 2 Women and the Church

1. Rick Warren (@RickWarren), "My Apology to Christian Women," Twitter (now X), June 10, 2023, 3:49 p.m., https://twitter.com/RickWarren/status/1667620086251925505?lang=en.

2. Sarah Bessey, *Jesus Feminist: An Invitation to Revisit the Bible's View of Women* (New York: Howard Books, 2013), 50.

3. Bill Johnson, *Face to Face with God: The Ultimate Quest to Experience His Presence* (Lake Mary, FL: Charisma House, 2007), 203–4.

4. Kenneth E. Bailey, *Jesus through Middle Eastern Eyes: Cultural Studies in the Gospels* (Downers Grove, IL: IVP Academic, 2008), 220.

5. Ezra Cohen, ed., "Women and Talmud Torah," Sefaria, accessed August 17, 2024, https://www.sefaria.org/sheets/103477.38?lang=bi&with=all&lang2=en.

6. Craig S. Keener, *The IVP Bible Background Commentary: New Testament*, 2nd ed. (Downers Grove, IL: IVP Academic, 2014), 208.

7. Katia Adams, *Equal: What the Bible Says about Women, Men, and Authority* (Colorado Springs: David C. Cook, 2019), 56.

8. Philip B. Payne, *Man and Woman, One in Christ: An Exegetical and Theological Study of Paul's Letters* (Grand Rapids: Zondervan, 2009), 119.

9. I. Howard Marshall, "Mutual Love and Submission in Marriage: Colossians 3:18–19 and Ephesians 5:21–33," in *Discovering Biblical Equality: Complementarity without Hierarchy*, ed. Ronald W. Pierce, Rebecca Merrill Groothuis, and Gordon D. Fee (Downers Grove, IL: IVP Academic, 2005), 186.

10. Adams, *Equal*, 177.

Chapter 3 Managing Expectations

1. *Barbie*, directed by Greta Gerwig (Warner Bros., 2023).

2. Henry Cloud (@drhenrycloudofficial), "You only owe others what you have promised, not what they expect because it's what they want," Instagram, January 30, 2024, https://www.instagram.com/p/C2vgu pmOyn3/.

3. Brené Brown, *Dare to Lead: Brave Work. Tough Conversations. Whole Hearts* (New York: Random House, 2018), 48.

4. John Mark Comer, *The Ruthless Elimination of Hurry: How to Stay Emotionally Healthy and Spiritually Alive in the Chaos of the Modern World* (Colorado Springs: WaterBrook, 2019), 25.

Chapter 4 Our Greatest Enemy

1. Bill Johnson, "When we believe a lie, we empower the liar," Facebook, June 20, 2014, https://www.facebook.com/BillJohnson Ministries/posts/when-we-believe-a-lie-we-empower-the-liar/10152 344398283387.

2. Dr. Seuss, *Happy Birthday to You!* (New York: Random House, 1959), 45.

Chapter 5 Destroying Jealousy and Competition

1. Cyprian of Carthage, "On Jealousy and Envy," Catholic Library Project, accessed August 18, 2024, https://catholiclibrary.org/library /view?docId=Synchronized-EN/anf.Cyprian.OnjealousyandEnvy.en .html&chunk.id=00000011.

2. Louisa M. Alcott, *Little Women* (New York: Penguin Group, 1989), 75.

3. Bill Johnson, *Hosting the Presence: Unveiling Heaven's Agenda* (Shippensburg, PA: Destiny Image, 2012), 61.

4. Bill Johnson, "Whatever you gain through self promotion you'll have to sustain through self promotion. When our promotion comes from God, He sustains it," Facebook, September 15, 2014, https://www.facebook.com/BillJohnsonMinistries/posts/whatever-you-gain-through-self-promotion-youll-have-to-sustain-through-self-prom/10152543247808387.

Chapter 6 More Than Me and Jesus

1. Roger E. Olson, *The Mosaic of Christian Belief: Twenty Centuries of Unity and Diversity*, 2nd ed. (Downers Grove, IL: IVP Academic, 2016), 317.

2. Brené Brown, *Daring Greatly: How the Courage to Be Vulnerable Transforms the Way We Live, Love, Parent, and Lead* (New York: Avery, 2012), 112.

3. Amanda J. Rose and Karen D. Rudolph, "A Review of Sex Differences in Peer Relationship Processes: Potential Trade-offs for the Emotional and Behavioral Development of Girls and Boys," *Psychological Bulletin* 132, no. 1 (January 2006): 98–131, https://doi.org/10.1037/0033-2909.132.1.98.

Chapter 7 Healthy Female Relationships

1. Jacob M. Vigil, "Asymmetries in the Friendship Preferences and Social Styles of Men and Women," *Human Nature* 18, no. 2 (June 2007): 143–61.

Chapter 8 Ending Codependency

1. Melody Beattie, *Codependent No More: How to Stop Controlling Others and Start Caring for Yourself* (Center City, MN: Hazelden, 2009), 53, Kindle.

2. Robert Subby, "Inside the Chemically Dependent Marriage: Denial and Manipulation," in *Co-Dependency, An Emerging Issue* (Hollywood, FL: Health Communications, 1984), 26.

3. Beattie, *Codependent No More*, 53.

4. Henry Cloud and John Townsend, *Boundaries: When to Say Yes, How to Say No to Take Control of Your Life* (Grand Rapids: Zondervan, 1992), 32.

5. Cloud and Townsend, *Boundaries*, 31.

6. Cloud and Townsend, *Boundaries*, 147.

7. Timothy Keller, *Counterfeit Gods: The Empty Promises of Money, Sex, and Power, and the Only Hope That Matters* (New York: Penguin Books, 2009), xx.

Chapter 9 Kick Fear Out of the Way

1. Kris Vallotton, *Destined to Win* (Nashville: Thomas Nelson, 2017), 140.

2. Thomas Jefferson to John Adams, April 8, 1816, in *Memoir, Correspondence, and Miscellanies: From the Papers of Thomas Jefferson*, 2nd ed. (Boston: Gray and Bowen, 1830), 4:271.

3. Corrie ten Boom, *God Is My Hiding Place* (Minneapolis: Chosen Books, 2021), 38.

4. Bill Johnson, *The Way of Life: Experiencing the Culture of Heaven on Earth* (Shippensburg, PA: Destiny Image, 2019), 79.

Chapter 10 Woman, You Can Lead!

1. John C. Maxwell, "A great leader's courage to fulfill his vision comes from passion, not position," Twitter (now X), February 9, 2021, 7:00 a.m., https://x.com/thejohncmaxwell/status/1359109914 694737920.

2. *Merriam-Webster*, s.v. "leadership," accessed June 28, 2024, https://www.merriam-webster.com/dictionary/leadership.

3. *American Dictionary of the English Language*, s.v. "leader," accessed June 28, 2024, https://webstersdictionary1828.com/Diction ary/leader.

4. John Maxwell, *Life Wisdom: Quotes from John Maxwell: Insights on Leadership* (Nashville: B&H Publishing Group, 2014), 152.

5. Alice H. Eagly and Steven J. Karau, "Role Congruity Theory of Prejudice toward Female Leaders," *Psychological Review* 109, no. 3 (July 2002): 573–98, https://doi.org/10.1037/0033-295X.109.3.573.

6. Alice H. Eagly, Mona G. Makhijani, and Bruce G. Klonsky, "Gender and the Evaluation of Leaders: A Meta-Analysis," *Psychological Bulletin* 111, no. 1 (1992): 3–22, https://doi.org/10.1037/0033 -2909.111.1.3.

7. Mansi P. Joshi and Amanda B. Diekman, "'My Fair Lady?' Inferring Organizational Trust from the Mere Presence of Women in Leadership Roles," *Personality and Social Psychology Bulletin* 48, no. 8 (August 2022): 1220–37, https://doi.org/10.1177/01461672211035957.

8. James Gilchrist Lawson, ed., "Prayer," in *Cyclopedia of Religious Anecdotes* (New York: Fleming H. Revell, 1923), 303.

Chapter 11 Apostello—A Vision for the Future

1. David Kinnaman and Mark Matlock, *Faith for Exiles: 5 Ways for a New Generation to Follow Jesus in Digital Babylon* (Grand Rapids: Baker Books, 2019), 113.

2. Kinnaman and Matlock, *Faith for Exiles*, 109–142.

Jessika Tate is an international speaker, missionary, author, and unashamed coffee lover who has been traveling the world preaching the gospel for over fifteen years in some of the darkest places on earth. She loves to preach the gospel with humor and authenticity and is passionate about inspiring people to fall in love with Jesus, equipping the church to fully yield their lives and walk in the power of the Holy Spirit.

Jessika is the founder of Yielded Ministries, a nonprofit organization that focuses on providing aid and advocacy for communities in unjust and vulnerable situations. In addition to Yielded, she is the leader of the Apostello Movement, which uses Bible studies, retreats, internships, and trainings to equip the next generation of church leaders. She currently resides in Franklin, Tennessee, where she gathers young people weekly to disciple them and teach them the power of kingdom family.

She graduated with a bachelor's degree from Texas Tech University (Wreck 'em!) and from Global Awakening Theological Seminary with her master's degree in pastoral care.

When she's not traveling or preaching, she loves to get out in the beauty of the Tennessee hills to go hiking, kayaking, or trail running.

You can follow Jessika, as well as Yielded Ministries and the Apostello Movement, on social media:

 @JessikaTate | @YieldedGlobal | @ApostelloMovement

 ApostelloMovement.com /Jessika.Tate.5